FOLLOWING
JESUS

FOLLOWING
JESUS

a non-religious guidebook for the spiritually hungry

by dave roberts

[RELEVANTBOOKS]

Published by Relevant Books
A division of Relevant Media Group, Inc.

www.relevantbooks.com
www.relevantmediagroup.com

© 2004 by Relevant Media Group

Design: Relevant Solutions
www.relevant-solutions.com

Relevant Books is a registered trademark of Relevant Media
Group, Inc., and is registered in the U.S. Patent and Trademark
Office.

Materials in chapters one and twelve appear in a modified form
in *Red Moon Rising*, by Dave Roberts and Pete Greig (Kingsway
Publications, 2004).

For information or bulk sales:
RELEVANT MEDIA GROUP, INC.
POST OFFICE BOX 951127
LAKE MARY, FL 32795
407-333-7152

Library of Congress Control Number: 2003096209
International Standard Book Number: 0-9729276-3-8

04 05 06 07 9 8 7 6 5 4 3 2 1

Printed in the United States of America

To Pete Greig, Lee Jackson, Andy Hawthorne,
Andy Whisker, Les Moir, and Mark Bowness.

Followers of Jesus. Dangerous people—every one of them.

CONTENTS

INTRODUCTION

THE VISION IS JESUS

There's a poem that's gone around the world. It was written on a 24-7 prayer room wall at three in the morning by Pete Greig.[1] Somebody wrote it down and emailed it to a friend. Soon people were making music for it, memorizing it, and chanting lines from it in giant stadiums. It touched the hearts of many, not least the underground Chinese Church, who circulated it to their members.

It's a sweeping overview of the kind of radical commitment many yearn for. At its heart is one line that arrested me: "The vision is Jesus—obsessively, dangerously, undeniably Jesus."

I was stopped by this line, but I was started on a journey of discovery about Jesus by another sentence. I was due to meet with friends to talk, pray, and worship. What were we going to talk about? If Jesus spent time getting to know people and befriending them, He must have eaten with them—why not talk about that?

We talked for hours that night about Jesus and food. It seemed too mundane. Shouldn't we be talking about something uplifting like "God's End Time Timetable" or "Seven Steps to Personal

Holiness"?

I've not been quite the same since that conversation. Jesus was always eating: the wedding at Cana; Zacchaeus; the road to Emmaus; the Last Supper; the feeding of the five thousand; a fish meal after the resurrection. The scandal of it was that He was eating with publicans and sinners, unholy people and friends of the enemies of faith. He talked about food and banquets in His parables. The mundane played an important role in the life of the sublime one.

I started to read more about His life and the everyday details of it. He ate with those He shouldn't have and in doing so, sent out two powerful signals. One, He was for the marginalized. Two, He refused to be bound by the extra 340 rules that the devout had added to the scriptures and that now regulated the life of a devout Pharisee.

Jesus was dangerous. Dangerous to the status quo, dangerous to the religious elite, dangerous to the complacent.

It's made me obsessive. Who was He? What did He mean as He taught? Who did He love? Who did He upset? Who was Jesus? Can we discover Him—or is He obscured by our rules, regulations, and biases? I've become obsessive about a dangerous man.

The vision is Jesus—obsessively, dangerously, undeniably Jesus.

I hope you discover the Jesus you never knew as you read the words of this book and that you decide to:

Follow Jesus.

THE MAGNIFICENCE OF JESUS
Do you feel that you've ever connected emotionally, intellectually, spiritually with the heart, the essence, the magnificence of what Jesus was and is and forever will be? I believe that we all need to

if we are going to follow Him. But it happens in many different ways as our life of faith unfolds.

I remember standing in the middle of an impassioned prayer gathering, wondering what I was doing there, suddenly struck by the serenity of someone waiting for prayer, quietly talking to God. How tender hearted she looked. Then the Spirit spoke, "Imagine what a tender hearted generation could do."

But what was the foundation of that tender heart? I had caught glimpses of it over the years. I had stood in a liturgical church as the minister intoned the communion prayer, which thanked God that He saw us "when we were still a long way off" and felt in an instant that moment of clarity and comprehension. God, through Jesus, loved me as much as the prodigal of the parable in the Bible.

Another day I sat down to look for the dominant tone in Jesus' life. I read the "red letter" sections containing only His words in every Gospel. I read them in one sitting, revelling in His words to the exclusion of all else. It was a moment of confrontation. There were wise responses, prophetic anger at injustice, and hard warnings for the religious elite, but how did Jesus treat the ordinary men and women? We know the words He brought, but what characterized the messenger?

It was inescapable: He welcomed the needy; He spoke graciously to them; He healed their diseases; He offered them wisdom for living; He offered His life as a means to bring forgiveness; He destroyed the works of the evil one through His death on the cross and resurrection into eternal life.

Jesus, I discovered, confronts our methods, attitudes, and practices. What should we do on the Sabbath? Who should we spend time socially with? Is eating with people, praying for them, and declaring God's peace in their lives a foundation for the relationship that enables us to tell them that God wants to rule and reign and to become the trademark that others see in their lives?[2]

Jesus was the relentless lover of humanity. Imagine a love as high as the heavens, deeper than the depths of the ocean, effortlessly stronger than the powers of darkness, sweeter than wine to a thirsty generation.

It's a love that provokes in us a sense of urgency. The urgency that impels me to write this book is that the powers of darkness are at work all around us, dividing families, alienating children, selling drugs, making obscene profits from legal drugs, killing babies, making designer babies ...

The list could go on and on, taking in our personal sin and wrongdoing and covering the culture shaping idolatries of celebrity, power, the body beautiful, and a self-centered sexual ethic.

I don't want to settle, faced with this, into my own private castle, living a life of quiet desperation, feeling inarticulate amid the babble of voices that seek to bring direction to people desperate for answers. I want to know how Jesus lived. How did God-made-flesh, Immanuel, God with us, live when He was here in bodily form? What can I discover that will help me lead a life now that is both human and holy?

How can I bring the presence of Jesus to the places I go and the people I'm with?

How can I let Jesus shape my values? What is it about Him and His life that will renew my mind and empower me to live like Him?

CHANGE MY WAY OF THINKING

God urges us to be renewed in the patterns of our thinking.[3] If we are to discover a faith that sustains and gives us the "word that sustains the weary," we may have to examine the patterns of our own thinking.[4]

Here are ten challenges that we must face. Ten patterns of thinking that need examination. Ten ideas that need the scrutiny of witness of the life of Jesus.

A church that's willing to examine its ideas, re-shape them in the light of Jesus life, and apply them 24/7/365 will change nations. But first we have to be offended by the life of Jesus. Are you ready to be offended? Are the ideas below legitimate or a diversion from the joy of following Jesus?

IDEA 1 This is an evil world full of evil people; we must be at a safe distance from them.

Jesus hadn't heard of this idea, or He wouldn't have allowed prostitutes to touch Him and tax collectors to feed Him.

IDEA 2 We should stand up and fight the godless enemies of our faith using every means possible.

Jesus didn't live His life in the light of this idea, or He wouldn't have healed the soldier who Peter attacked in the garden.

IDEA 3 We need instant decisions, instant answers, and instant breakthroughs.

Jesus took three years to train the disciples. We need miracle breakthroughs *and* steady reflective progress.

IDEA 4 If only we had a powerful speaker, revival would come.

Jesus' life and ministry touched all of the five senses. He used poetry, conversation, and short talks. Even the Sermon on the Mount only lasts about six to seven minutes.

IDEA 5 We can only do that which the Bible explicitly mentions.

There goes the church steeple, women's meetings, data projector, Sunday school, weddings, church choir, and the neighborhood.

IDEA 6 Guilt is a good spiritual motivator.

Jesus didn't come to promote guilt as a lifestyle, but merely as a bridge to a new life. Guilt is like brakes on a car. You use them to stop; you don't use them to steer. Our steering wheel is the words and deeds of Jesus.

IDEA 7 You must do this because I said it/God said it.

Jesus came to introduce us to the wisdom that shaped creation, not call for unthinking obedience.

IDEA 8 It's their own fault they're poor and needy.

Jesus didn't seem to have heard of this idea when He healed the lepers, favored the shepherds, welcomed the tax collectors, and conversed with the prostitutes. God didn't seem to have heard of this idea when He introduced the idea of the year of Jubilee, when debts were forgiven and land returned.

IDEA 9 Follow my rhetoric or you're a heretic.

Do our theological ideas fit all the evidence about Jesus' life, or could it be that we're half-right? Should we shun those who think differently? How did Jesus cope with having a militant political disciple like Simon the Zealot and Matthew, a tax collector and friend of the Roman enemies of the ordinary Israelite?

IDEA 10 Let's get elected and change the nation.

Did you notice Jesus getting elected? No, nor did I. Did He command us to pray for our rulers? Yes. Did He and His disciples meet with people from the political elite, such as Joseph of Arimathea and Nicodemus? Yes. Does God want to us to influence society and government? Yes. Can we legislate for moral change? No.

THE PROPHETIC CHALLENGE

It's all too easy to criticize. But sometimes the truth only emerges as a contrast to the present realities and the distorted views of Jesus and Christianity that we all sometimes have.

The theologian Walter Brueggemann, writing in *The Prophetic Imagination*, reminds his readers that we can't critique if we don't also energize with the Word of God.

If we want to know why the Christian Church has embraced the ideas above and is sometimes legalistic, power seeking, narrow-minded, unsympathetic, psychologically wounding, intolerant, separatist, and violent, we also need to know how it might conform itself to the life of Christ, or we'll simply breed cynicism in our hearts and the hearts of others.

What kind of church is it we're looking for? The Church I'm aspiring to, working toward, exploring in my mind, and seeking to implement will be:

Culturally present—not on the margins of society.

Gracious—even to those about whom we harbor the gravest doubts.

Sensitive—we all grow in faith in different ways and speeds.

Wise—the Bible is about life 24/7/365, not just about meetings.

Creative—Jesus did more than talk.

Joyful—being thankful as an intentional decision.

Compassionate—because we do what we see the Father doing.[5]

Upside-down—because a nation can be changed by ordinary people and extraordinary lives.

Each sentence has the seeds of prophetic challenge within it. Each sentence could undermine something you take to be the norm in your life or in the Church.

So are you ready to change your way of thinking?

Are you ready to ...

Follow Jesus?

Dave Roberts
info@tahilla.com
www.tahilla.com

1. You can discover more about this poem, "The Vision," in *Red Moon Rising*, Pete Greig and Dave Roberts (Relevant Books, 2003). This tells the story of how a 24-7 prayer movement is touching the youth of more than fifty nations.
2. Luke 10:5-9
3. Romans 12:1-2
4. Isaiah 50:4
5. John 5:19

1

REAL HOLY LIVING

Perhaps you've met the extremists: Susan Separate and Andy
Activist. You'll find them in most towns and in many churches.
See if you recognize them:

Susan is not one to be contradicted. This world is not her home;
she's just passing through. She is quite comfortable with her
church meetings and her Christian TV channels. She regrets
having to work in the world, but it does give her a chance to
witness. Her vocabulary is littered with spiritual jargon, and her
conversation is more Christian than Christ's. She worries that
she doesn't see more people come to Christ, but we do live at a
particularly godless time and the Lord is in control, so everything
will work out, even if we don't understand it all. Life would be
easier if she could meet a godly man, but that single life is very …
spiritual.

Susan is in cultural retreat, and she is perverting the biblical idea
of holiness.

Andy Activist is on a mission to rescue planet earth single-
handedly. He is going to save the lost, fight injustice, save the

whale, save the rain forest, and save the planet, and if you don't join in, you're just part of the problem. "What is the point," he enquires, "of hiding away in a church having prayer meetings when there are mouths to be fed, AIDS victims to be educated, broken hearts to be bound up, and rainforests to save?"

Andy is in cultural advance, but is losing his faith moorings as he increasingly denigrates the very things that would inform the compassion he seeks to exercise.

These are, of course, unfair caricatures, but I'm sure they sound familiar to us all. But they beg the question of whether it has to be an either/or choice between the spiritual and the mundane. Jesus didn't seem to see any tension between intimacy with God and a vigorous involvement in the everyday things of life.

Would it be possible to be culturally present and infused with true holiness?

Jesus was.

THE GOSPEL OF PRAYER
Luke, the writer of the third Gospel, is renowned for his eye for detail and historical accuracy. A golden thread running through Luke's Gospel is the private prayer life of Jesus. It's worth noting that the Gospel writers simply presumed the reader would have knowledge of the daily habits of prayer and blessings that marked the contemplative life of any devout Jew. Jesus and the disciples maintained such rhythms of prayer. But in addition, Jesus would often withdraw for solitary prayer:

- Luke 5:16—But Jesus often withdrew to lonely places and prayed.
- Luke 6:12—Jesus went out to a mountainside to pray and spent the night praying to God.
- Luke 9:18—Once when Jesus was praying in private and His disciples were with him …
- Luke 9:28—He took Peter, James and John with Him and

went up on to a mountain to pray.
- Luke 11:1—One day Jesus was praying in a certain place.
- Luke 22:39—Jesus went out as usual to the Mount of Olives. He withdrew, knelt down, and prayed.

Here was a man defined by intimacy with the Father. It was the indisputable key to all He did and all He said. He did not neglect the spiritual disciplines that fed the flame of love that characterized all He said and did.

THE WILDNESS OF THE ORDINARY

But Jesus wasn't a withdrawn, otherworldly spiritual mystic locked away in perpetual prayer. He embraced the justice and compassion tradition already declared by the prophets as the will of God. The prophet Amos warned about dishonest weights, selling the poor for footwear, and taking bribes to corrupt justice. He called out on behalf of God, "But let justice roll on like a river, righteousness like a never-failing stream!"[1] Jesus, as we will discover, echoed this call, but He made the very ordinary habits of His daily devotional life a springboard for countercultural involvement with humanity.

A quiet melody buried in the symphony of the Gospels carries the scandalous story of Jesus' eating habits. As we hear the stinging rebuke of the Pharisees regarding Jesus' willingness to eat with "publicans and sinners," we perhaps hear it through the ears of our experience of faith. Are we hearing the patronizing voice of the self-righteous? Are we hearing the voice that fears that too much time with a non-believer will pollute our minds? It leaves us ruefully shaking our heads about the proud Pharisees.

But the reality is that Jesus was undermining the rigid caste system of His day. He was mixing with the unclean. He was supposed to be a Messiah, but He wouldn't observe the rudimentary purity laws designed to produce a holy nation for God. The religious authorities had added more than 340 additional laws to the scripture. More than two-thirds of these related to food.

When you hear Jesus inviting himself to Zacchaeus' house, where it was inevitable He would eat, you're hearing the voice of revolt. The message is that God will be involved with people, even if they are in a group—tax collectors—deemed ritually unclean.

When you hear Jesus inviting the disciples to eat fish with Him after His resurrection, you're hearing a God who will remain involved in the everyday intimacies and patterns of life, even as this group of eleven are prepared to shape world civilization.

When you read the Gospels and note all the references to food, you discover a Savior who takes what we view as mundane, but the society of the time regarded as highly symbolic, and uses it as a sign of acceptance and a bridge to friendship, dialogue, and spiritual change.

He also let an unclean woman weep over His feet, when the expedient thing to have done was to ask her to find a local female sympathizer to counsel her. He touched the diseased, dead, or dying, rendering Himself unclean, but rendering them clean, healed, and forgiven.

AN INVITATION TO WORSHIP

Jesus was involved with people. He reminded His disciples that their involvement with people would be like an act of worship to Him, talking about a day when the King will say:

"For I was hungry and you gave me something to eat; I was thirsty and you gave me something to drink, I was a stranger and you invited me in. I needed clothes and you clothed me, I was sick and you looked after me. I was in prison and you came to visit me.' When the bewildered faithful ask when this happened he will reply: 'I tell you the truth, whatever you did for the least of these brothers of mine, you did for me.'"[2]

Jesus had made it clear from the very start of His public ministry that involvement with the poor and marginalized was to be a foundation of His message. Speaking shortly after His forty days in the wilderness, He announced to the Nazareth synagogue:

The Spirit of the Lord is upon me,
Because he has anointed me
To preach good news to the poor.[3]

It is clear Jesus wanted us to be involved with people. What has the Church done in response to this over the millennia? In the U.K., it is estimated that our 49,000 churches are involved in more than 144,000 social compassion projects (Oasis, Faithworks Survey, 2003). While sections of the Church may well live in the proverbial "holy huddle," isolated from the world and only "raiding" it for potential converts, the witness of history suggests that movements of revival and renewal, sparked by prayer, are the engines of Christian compassion for decades after the spiritual passion was at its height.

Timothy L. Smith, writing in *Revivalism and Social Reform*, reflected at length on the fruits of the 1857 prayer revival, which was to spark hundreds of thousands of conversions. A prayer meeting of six men became the foundation of a prayer movement that swept New York, America, Northern Ireland, and Scotland from 1857-1859. This involved thousands in daily or weekly prayer meetings and fueled the 1959 Ulster Revival.

He comments: "The prayer of all disciples, 'Thy kingdom come, Thy will be done on earth as it is in heaven' took on new significance as the soul winning impulse drove Christians into systematic efforts to relieve the miseries of the urban poor. Individual churches soon joined the inter-denominational societies in distributing food and clothing, finding employment, resettling children and providing medical aid .... The revival of 1858 was in many respects the harvest reaped from this gospel seed."[4]

Revivalists were active in the formation of caring institutions such as the Young Men's Christian Association (YMCA); Charles Finney and others were vigorous in their denunciation of slavery.

This is just the tip—writing about the roots of social compassion could fill up a book in itself.

Jesus was intimate with the Father in prayer. This gave Him, and will give us, the passion to continue whatever the odds, in "loving our neighbor" in whatever contexts God places us.

CULTURALLY PRESENT

The challenge for those who would seek to follow Jesus is this: Can we be in the world but not of it? Jesus, even as He prepared for the cross, prayed to the Father: "My prayer is not that you take them out of the world but that you protect them from the evil one."[5]

Jesus was present in the culture of His day but not in thrall to its values. Asking ourselves some questions may help us be the same.

How can we be separate but present?

The Scripture tells us to come "out from among them and be separate."[6] We are also encouraged to "love not the world."[7] For many, these two texts are enough to justify cutting themselves off from the world. The two verses need further explanation. Paul is writing to the Corinthians, who seemed fond of taking the grace of God for granted as they got drunk at the communion service and indulged their sexual passions outside of marriage. He urges them to stop mixing institutionally, or in formal relationships, with people of other religions and uses images of worship and marriage to bring the message home. He is urging them to be distinct and principled, not invisible and marginal.

The call to love not the world should also be seen as a call to look to God in Christ as the root of all wisdom and to find delight in Him. This is in contrast to believing in the thought patterns of the culture around us and having an idolatrous relationship with God's good gifts of fine food, beautiful creation, and sexuality. The Greek of the passage infers that it is the philosophy of the world that is to be avoided.

Scriptures such as these need to be read in the light of other scriptures. For God so loved the world that He sent His Son. His Son was constantly mixing with the wrong people. His disciples and followers remained in their conventional occupations as tent makers, fishermen, and tax collectors. They maintained friendship ties with the poor (Dorcas fed them), the needy, the widowed (the deacons were appointed to look after them), the rich (Lydia), and the learned (Paul debated with them in the marketplace). Their churches grew daily.

I believe that this growth was partly related to daily informal contact with non-Christians. Jesus practiced it. What other argument do we need?

What is our job in the world?

Why are we here? The book of Genesis suggests that we are to "fill the earth and subdue it." The creation mandate includes the encouragement to work and take care of creation.[8] We are stewards or keepers of creation and can view our role on this earth as an act of worship. Whatever our jobs in life, we can in some way contribute to the health and good of our community and the land in which we live. We will be culture formers, using our God-given creativity to reflect Him in the way we do our jobs, raise our families, and treat other people, and in the music, poetry, and art we create.

While we will be rejected by some and they will separate us out from them as Jesus warned, there seems to be no New Testament precedent for creating closed communities isolated from the rest of society. The Christians remained involved in the everyday lives of their towns and cities even when they withdrew from the pagan temple worship.

This is inferred by Paul's discussion about eating meat offered to idols. He clearly indicates that he believes that no harm will come to those who eat it. He further suggests that you are innocent if you did not know it had been offered in this way. He cautions against knowingly eating it, lest you be seen to be giving credence to the pagan belief system. The very fact that he is offering these guidelines for friendships with pagan people would seem to infer that the believers remained involved in the day to day lives of their communities.[9]

Holiness is a heart attitude. It is not a mere avoidance of sin. Jesus cautioned against the complacency that looked at sin in a forensic legal way and encouraged people to examine the attitudes that fueled sin.[10] A lifetime of discovery of the attitudes that motivated Jesus will change our hearts and incline us toward an instinctive holiness that is as natural as breathing. This book is a simple description of what I've discovered so far.

IN COMMUNITY, FOR OUR COMMUNITY

We have a responsibility to be salt and light in the communities we find ourselves in.[11] Within those communities we will have four spheres of influence:

- Our family—the place of most influence.
- Our workplace—where our lives are on show daily.
- Our neighborhood—the people we greet in the street, the people at the local shops, the people who clean our streets and deliver goods.
- Our voluntary associations—the friends we choose to be with, the community activities we choose to surport.

The weakness we often suffer is that we regard work as a necessary evil, and the neighborhood as full of sinners, and we often have no community links or non-Christian friends. We are holy on our own.

Changing that involves examining our view of life in the light of the Bible and making a deliberate choice to connect with those who do not know Jesus.

We are here to make and lead culture. We are here to bless our communities. We are here to be a prophetic voice when injustice or evil seek to have their sway. We are not here to survive. This is not God's waiting room. We can make a difference whether we are in conventional positions of power or not—the final chapter of this book will describe how we can engage with society and influence every sphere of life.

We can do none of this alone. It's instructive that Jesus had one close friend, three in His inner circle, twelve as His disciples, seventy-two as His followers, and 500-plus who witnessed His resurrection. We cannot be holy and present in the culture in isolation. We need each other. We learn from one and other. We are accountable to one and other.

We need to follow Jesus together.

FOR FURTHER READING:

Pete Greig, *Awakening Cry* (Kingsway, 2004)
Alvin J. Schmidt, *Under the Influence* (Zondervan, 2001). This book examines the role of Christianity in shaping hospitals, education, science, human rights, art and architecture, workplace justice, and several other important spheres.

1. Amos 5:24
2. Matthew 25:31-40
3. Luke 4:18
4. Timothy L. Smith, *Revivalism and Social Reform* (John Hopkins University Press, 1989).
5. John 17:15
6. 2 Corinthians 6:17
7. 1 John 2:15
8. Genesis 1:26, 2:15
9. 1 Corinthians 10
10. Matthew 5:22
11. Matthew 5:13-14

2

JESUS OUTSIDE THE BOX:
DISCOVERING THE PARADOXES

They had to get rid of Eric the Messiah. It wasn't easy. His image was everywhere. Bedroom walls, Sunday school classrooms, church entrances. He had to go. They were creating him in their image.

People were mistaking him for Jesus, the King of the Jews and the Savior of mankind. Jesus, a man born into a Semitic family. You wondered what kind of genetic quirk there would have to be in the family line of King David—from which His mother came— for Him to be a blue-eyed, blond-haired Nordic Messiah.

Slowly but surely Eric has disappeared. Church Sunday school art departments purged his image from their hard drives, and the visual depictions of the Savior of mankind stumbled toward realism.

How do you and I view Jesus? Do we perceive Him as human or divine, tender or tough, a comforter or a prophet, a man of the people or a member of the elite? Do we want our Jesus to be neat and predictable? Are we trying to create Him in our image?

It helps if He is neat and predictable, if He's an either/or person. We can be militant and confrontational if Jesus is one-dimensional.

SPIRITUALLY CORRECT IDOLATRY

Perhaps you've met a few militants in your time. "The problem with society today is sex/drugs/rock 'n' roll/communism/multinational capitalism/Islam/blacks/whites/Catholics/Protestants/the Christian right/homosexuals/heterosexuals."

Maybe you've met their church cousins. "The Church would be healthier if we prayed more/sung more/had more of the Spirit/had less of the tele-evangelists/were more socially aware."

The prophets of "if only" sometimes nag us into examining issues that we need to confront. If we're not careful, however, we become terminal whiners, always finding fault, never quite satisfied, and perpetually angry with someone.

Being spiritually correct can become a kind of idolatry. Christian writer Dietrich Bonhoeffer described a "wish dream" mentality, where our idea of how things should be becomes more important than Jesus, more important than people, a personal crusade.

He describes it this way: "He who loves the dream of a community more than the Christian community itself becomes a destroyer of the latter, even though his personal intentions may be ever so honest and earnest and sacrificial."[1]

Christian counselor Ken Sharp describes how our idealism can become a "wish dream." He comments: "Hopes twisted become false hopes."

Togetherness—becomes a wish for no differences, conflict, or diversity.

Acceptance—grows into a demand for no criticism, no negatives, and no confrontation.

Harmony—emerges as an attempt to feel no anger, conflict, or arousal.

Love—turns into a need to control, manipulate, and dominate.

Adequacy—is expressed as a belief that tender, sad, or painful feelings must be suppressed or denied.

Success—can make one afraid of failure, frightened of facing any imperfections.[2]

ONE EXPLANATION SYNDROME

Our discomfort with an inability to keep life tidy is not confined to our idealistic goals in life and often spills over into our analysis of culture. We want life to be simple and all the explanations to be brief. We would argue: "Young people today are having more sex because of the relentless diet of sexuality fed to them via film, TV, and literature. Clean up popular culture, and sexual purity will increase."

The reality is messier. Popular media does give people "permission" to be more sexually active, but sexual freedom has also become the norm in society because:

1. Family breakdown and the loss of community leave many desperately lonely. Sex gives a sense of belonging and intimacy.

2. The Church has often portrayed sexuality in a deeply negative way. The absence of a healthy view of Christian sexuality until recent times means that many Christians have only had negative things to say about sex. People rebel against a negative, joyless, and ultimately non-biblical view. Sexuality is a wonderful gift of God within the marriage relationship.

3. Changes in wealth patterns, social mobility, and housing availability give people more opportunity to experiment sexually, without risking the instant wrath of parents or community.

4. People have always been ready to use God's good gift as an idol. They take a good thing, erotic love, and make it the center of their existence and identity. The rejection of God's wisdom and authority within our culture means that people have had to learn by trial and error, rather than accepting the underlying wisdom that had prevailed for nearly two millennia. They soon discover why God set boundaries on erotic love. He wants to protect our physical, social, and emotional health from venereal disease, dashed hopes, and absent parents.

So while the underlying root of the sexual freedom of the last forty years is a self-centered ethic, many other things have contributed. There is no one single cause.

We find this in the history of God's relationship with mankind. Christian writers John Peck and Charles Strohmer are wary of the "one explanation syndrome." A marriage fails, and it's because the husband had an affair. A teenager is delinquent because both parents work. In both cases, however, there are often several reasons.

If we transfer our attention to the history of the people of Israel and their quest to enter the Promised Land, we might simply want to say that their tendency to get involved in grumbling and idolatry slowed their progress.

Peck and Strohmer find five reasons:

1. Like several other tribes, they didn't have iron chariots and couldn't occupy the plains as a result (Judges 1:19).

2. They weren't ready to respond to the Canaanite religion—there was a danger that they would be drawn in by it (Judges 1:28; 2:3).

3. They saw themselves as losers. If God kept giving them land by miraculous intervention, they would never learn to defend themselves (Judges 2:22; 3:5).

4. The failure of their faith. They simply did not believe they were going to receive the Promised Land as promised (Judges 3:7).

5. If they had been too successful too quick, they would not have had the resources to maintain the land, and the ecological balance of man, beast, and plant would have been upset (Deuteronomy 7: 22).[3]

How can this insight help us as we seek to understand or follow Jesus? Whatever stage of our faith journey we are at, whether we're merely curious about Jesus or focused on imitating His life, we will probably have picked up fragments, one-liners we associate with His name.

Gentle Jesus, meek and mild, is one. I once sat in a restaurant and heard a man at the next table tell his friends, "I prefer churches where they just talk about God. Jesus was basically a hippie." Here was one explanation syndrome at work, reducing a rich and varied life to a sneering label.

Jesus' life won't be captured in single line explanations. There is so much more. He doesn't always lend Himself to either/or answers. But a part of us recoils from the idea. We don't feel comfortable with paradox. We're wary of any suggestion that there are multiple explanations for a situation. We want our truth to be straightforward.

Spend a few hours on the Internet looking for sites about truth and heresy, doctrine and apostasy, and you'll find yourself walking through a maze of claims, counter claims, conspiracy theories, and impassioned warnings that your nation is under judgment because of the rise of sin/freemasonry/another brand of Christianity/a specific named preacher who is deceiving the elect.

Wary as we may be of this single-minded ministry of accusation, we will be cautious about compromise. For example, I do not believe all roads lead to God. I do believe in absolute truth. I think we have been given ten commandments, not ten suggestions.

But the reality is this: We are all human, and however hard we try, we will never quite have the truth neatly packaged. How are we to relate to others in the light of this? I practice what I call "principled tolerance." I sometimes spend time with people who may have a different view of biblical prophecy, baptism, or the role of women preachers to the one I hold. My only concern at that time is: What do they think of Jesus?

Do they believe He was the Son of God? Do they believe that He lived among us so that we could learn from His life? Do they believe that He died and rose again? Do they believe that our rebellion against God can be forgiven and that God will empower us by the Holy Spirit to live like Jesus?

Nobody pretends that we agree on the other issues. No one is being forced to change their perspective in the name of unity. We may well debate our perspectives. I may even feel that some views are quite destructive. It just seems more likely that people will change their thinking if I treat them with dignity and affirm what we can agree on.

I believe that Jesus defies our neat categories. I believe we need to be idealistic and patient. I believe we need to think twice when examining any situation. I believe we need to be committed to our ideas but treat those who don't share them with dignity.

I believe all of this because I believe this is what we discover in the life of Jesus.

1. Dietrich Bonhoeffer, *Life Together* (SCM Press, 1954).
2. *http://www.dallas.net/~irvingcc/sessionfeb98.html*
3. John Peck, Charles Strohmer, *Uncommon Sense: God's Wisdom for Our Complex and Changing World* (SPCK, 2001).

3

MEEK AND MILD

Gentle Jesus, meek and mild. It's a distortion, but a pervasive one; such is the power of song and poetry. But it's dangerous because it is simply not true.

There were times when He was meek. He was meek the day He walked through a hostile crowd that was bent on throwing Him over a cliff. He was meek when He healed the soldier slashed by the fiery Peter. He was meek when He carried the cross toward His death. He was meek when they placed the crown of thorns upon His head.

Jesus chose not to rise up in anger on these occasions, although He could have called ten thousand angels to His side and destroyed those who taunted Him with one word.

There were times when He chose to be meek.

But He was never mild. He was born into conflict and remained in it for the whole of His life. His family had to flee from a vengeful king; He came from a town that had a bad reputation; He jousted with the devil in the desert; He frequently exchanged words with the religious groups of the day. He risked life and reputation by spending time with housefulls of tax collectors and in the company of known prostitutes. He risked the wrath of thousands of people in Jericho by asking Himself to someone's house. He was not condemned to die on the cross because He was mild. He was sent there because He was wild.

Wild enough to turn over the tables of those who were fleecing the faithful as they came to the temple to worship. Wild enough to embrace the hated neighbors (Samaritans). Wild enough to eat with publicans and sinners. Wild enough to question the laws of the day which said you weren't to heal on the Sabbath. Wild enough to touch the unclean leper.

Jesus was meek and wild.

Are you comfortable with that paradox?

It is a challenge to our normal either/or mind-set. Is it possible to believe that Jesus' life was full of both/and tensions? Was He a comforter and a prophet, a tough man with a tender heart, someone who valued tradition but undermined tradition? What does the plain record of Scripture tell us?

I can believe that the life of Jesus was marked by paradox, because His very existence seems paradoxical to the ordinary mind. It's not hard to believe that He was a good man who God "adopted." That keeps Him human. It's not hard to believe He was God. Surely only God could have been as holy, perfect, and wise as Jesus. Surely our earthly humanity could not have soiled His divinity.

Jesus was human—easy to believe. Jesus was God—easy to believe. Jesus was both human and divine—much bigger challenge.

But that's what the scriptural record implies: He laid aside His majesty and came and lived among us.[1] He worked with His father as a carpenter. He fell asleep in boats during storms. He ate, He wept, He cried out in anguish as the time of His trial approached. He was moved with compassion for His friends Lazarus, Mary, and Martha.

Jesus was very human.

But Jesus was divine. His earthly mother Mary was impregnated by the Divine. Jesus was the Son of God. He talked to his Father constantly. He regularly used the term Father to describe God. In the Old Testament, this only happens forty times. In the New Testament, the figure is 260.

Jesus talked to the Father in prayer, using the term in every prayer, except in His cry of anguish on the cross as He lamented being "forsaken."

The record of His baptism suggests that God spoke from heaven and declared "This is my son, whom I love; with him I am well pleased."[2]

The record of His life speaks of His authority over the elements of nature. He walked on the water.[3] He rebuked the wind and the raging waters, and they became calm.[4]

He rose from the dead, was seen by more than 500 witnesses, and extended His nail-pierced hands to the doubting disciple Thomas.

How do we reconcile His divinity and His humanity? How could they co-exist? It may be helpful to reflect on the fact that once you concede that this complex universe had a Creator, it's not too hard to conceive of the place of the miraculous and unusual.

One writer in Eastbourne won't resolve the issues that surround that co-existence in the pages of a book such as this. Church councils have debated it for millennia. The exact nature of it is at the heart of the difference between the Orthodox churches and the rest of Christendom. Suffice it to say that the debate has been long because most involved in it want to do justice to the reality of the record of Jesus' life, and to resist the temptation to simply believe that He was either human or divine.

If we allow for the reality of the human/divine in the person of Jesus, what other tensions might we allow?

JESUS LOVED TRADITION;
JESUS UNDERMINED TRADITION

Everything about Jesus' life spoke of Him being deeply rooted in the culture of the Israelites to whom He spoke. So much of what He said was reflective of His respect for tradition. Here are some snapshots—a small cross-section of a huge body of evidence. When Jesus was challenged by the teacher of the law as to how he might inherit eternal life, Jesus asked a question designed to remind him of the daily prayer patterns of the Jews, one of which started and ended with passages from Deuteronomy 5 and 6. It was with these that the teacher responded.[5]

As the time of His death approached, He took the disciples to Jerusalem for the Passover meal. This symbolic meal was part of the spoken and acted history tradition of the Israelite people. Jesus was to transform it from the story of a nation's deliverance to a symbol of the deliverance of mankind. But He remained immersed in the tradition.

He told them to look out for a man carrying a water pitcher. The significance of the pitcher relates to the fact that it would signify that the man was devout and was preparing his house for the forthcoming Passover in the traditional way. The extended drama of this meal, lost in our short and minimalist versions, is the symbolic nature of the food, every prayer said, and every action undertaken during the meal.

The lamb had been cooked in the quickest way. Bread was baked without yeast. The Passover meal represented the story of those preparing to leave in haste. The bitter herbs represented the wild vegetables they snatched from the roadside to still their growing hunger. The reddish sauce reminded them of their forced labor under Pharaoh. The wine symbolized the joy of escape, the intoxication of gratitude to the Almighty.

At the end of the meal, the disciples and Jesus sang a hymn from the "Hallel" section of Psalms 114-118. The Passover meal was an acted out memory that helped shape the identity of all who participated in it.

There are many other small clues about Jesus and tradition. Jesus attended the feast in Jerusalem with His parents, spoke in the synagogue, observed the prayer patterns of His time, and participated in the everyday traditions of His time.

He publicly declared that He had not come to destroy the law but to fulfill it.[6] Jesus had no problem with basic commands of God revealed in the first five books of the Bible (Torah). But on the occasions when He clashed with the religious authorities of the day, He was usually ignoring the hedge of laws that the priests had built around the Torah. Jesus healed a crippled woman on the Sabbath, but was criticized for doing so. Jesus reminded the crowd that animals would be tended and rescued from harm on the Sabbath, and human beings deserved the same.[7]

He pointed out that it is always lawful to do good on the Sabbath. Elsewhere He pressed home the point by reminding His listeners that the Sabbath was a means for humankind to rest, and that it had not been instituted to provide a test of holiness.[8]

The Apostle Paul commented on information about the resurrection and the nature of the communion meal by referring to the fact these had become traditions among the early Church.[9]

Tradition kills when it feels like an obligation, but when viewed as a means of service, connection, and remembrance, it can be a joy and a comfort. What role might tradition have in your life? Are there everyday rhythms of friendship that help anchor you in your community—regular meals, gatherings for coffee, sporting events? Are there small rituals of faith that will keep your connection with Jesus alive—prayer, weeks of prayer, and family prayer? Are there annual events that present an opportunity to gather with like-minded people?

There are myriad traditions that will create a sense of belonging in this world for you. I'm loathe to describe them, lest it seems prescriptive on my part.

I encourage you think of tradition as being like a metal frame. It's solid and carefully designed. You can climb inside it and hide and let it become a cage. But you can climb on it, let it give you support, and view the world from the top of it.

And as you'll discover elsewhere in these pages, tradition can be a rich source of wisdom, to be followed because it enriches life, not merely because we feel we ought to.

Jesus loved the wisdom behind the traditions He observed, but shied away from those who sought to ensure they were followed by imposing hundreds of minor rules. Does any of this feel familiar to you?

Jesus, the man of paradox, loved wise tradition, but also undermined the traditions of men.

JESUS WAS A COMFORTER; JESUS WAS A PROPHET

A pattern of hope is in Jesus' dealings with the lost, broken, and marginalized people whom He met.

Jesus had announced His mission in the synagogue by declaring He had come to bring good news to the poor, freedom for the captives, sight for the blind, and the release of the oppressed.[10]

To the woman caught in adultery, who had come so close to death, He said: "Woman, where are they? Has no one condemned you?"

"No one, sir," she said. "Then neither do I condemn you," Jesus declared. "Go now and leave your life of sin."[11]

Jesus took time for those deemed not important even by His disciples. They had rebuked the parents who sought Jesus' touch for their child, but Jesus called the children to Him with the words: "Do not hinder them, for the kingdom of God belongs to such as these."[12]

Jesus was an emotional man. His life was not all cool logic and careful theology. Outside the town of Nain, He met the funeral cortege of a loved son, mourned by his widowed mother. When he saw her, His heart went out to her, and He told her not to cry. He spoke with the authority of one who had been there at the creation of the universe, and life returned to the young man's body.

He also looked at the ordinary detail of people's lives and sought to meet their mundane needs. Aware that those who had spent three days listening to Him might be hungry and would need strength for their journey home, He had compassion on them and performed a miracle with fish and bread that meant four thousand men were fed.[13]

Jesus comforted the afflicted, but He also afflicted the comfortable.

Faced with the harsh judgments of the teachers of the law, He wondered if they would ever be satisfied and whether they would always find fault. In their eyes John the Baptist's abstinence and diet meant He was demonized. But Jesus, who ate bread and drunk wine, was condemned as a glutton and a drunkard. "Wisdom," He warned, would be "proved right by all her children."

He warned His own disciples that following Him would mean daily sacrifice and self-denial.[14] He invited the expert on the law to consider the possibility that a Samaritan, the despised neighbor of the Israelite people, might be the one He was being called to love and emulate. He described the king as a fox.[15]

Jesus seemed to care little for popular opinion, warning healed people not to gossip about what had happened to them, risking the wrath of the whole city of Jericho by visiting the tax collector whom everyone hated, and musing that some of the crowds following were spiritual thrill seekers from a "wicked generation."[16]

This prophetic confrontation was a hallmark of Jesus' words and deeds and will echo throughout every chapter of this book. Are you ready to confront systems of thought with the challenge of the life and words of Jesus? Are you willing to express an unpopular opinion and face the anger and misrepresentation of your motives that will result? Can you live with the tension of seeking to balance that mental toughness with a gracious kindness to people seeking to make sense of their lives and circumstances?

It is vital that you do. Impatience and a judgmental attitude are the curse of the prophet who doesn't internalize the wisdom of the whole of Jesus' life.

Are you willing to embrace the paradox of grace and justice?

JESUS WAS TENDER; JESUS WAS TOUGH

Jesus' life is a challenge to men. If we have been raised in a culture of emotional concealment and taught that the manly thing to do was hide our feelings, then the emotional transparency of Jesus will be an unsettling irritant. It'll help close the spiritual doors of a man's heart if it isn't balanced with the reality of Jesus' boldness, bravery, lack of compromise, and willingness to stand up to the dominant voices in the culture to which He came.

Standing before the tomb of his friend Lazarus, Jesus wept. Looking over Jerusalem, He once again wept as He told of the pain that would be the lot of the people because they had not heeded the message that would bring them peace.[17]

The heartbeat of God sounds in the steady reminders we get of Jesus' compassion. We see the acts of compassion, but can we begin to feel the deep emotions that precipitated them?

It seems He was feeling their pain and alienation, understanding that they were harassed and helpless, unsure of whom to look to for leadership or protection. He found it impossible to ignore sickness, often making His first task the healing of the sick. He healed two blind men and took the risk of touching the unclean leper as He was moved with compassion in response to their heartfelt requests.[18]

Jesus was a tenderhearted man.

But what kind of toughness did it take to hear people attribute your miracles to the devil, to walk through crowds ready to throw you over a cliff, or to endure the lashes that should never have been given to an innocent man?

What kind of man would drive out those who exploited the poor in the temple courtyards, turning over their tables as He did so? What kind of man would die the slow death of suffocation to which hanging from the cross sentenced you?

What kind of man would endure the wrenching pain as the blood seeped from His side, the strength in His arms failing as his torn wrists shot pain through His body, but still speak words of kindness to a dying thief?

What kind of man would return to a group of men that had betrayed Him and make the most verbal traitor the leader of His new community? What kind of man would step nimbly around the verbal traps laid by His opponents, seeking to get Him to disagree with the law of Moses, or the tax laws of the day?[19]

Not a weak man, not a timid man, not a man who lacked

25

principles, and not a man whose life was held captive by the opinions of others.

Jesus was tough because He was compassionate. One led to the other. He had come to take captivity captive. He had come to release the oppressed.

If we only ever speak of the tender Jesus, we will slip into sentimentality. If we only ever speak of the Jesus who challenged human hearts, we will end up sounding shrill. If we speak of both, we can bring words that will sustain and nourish a spiritually hungry, weary, and brokenhearted generation.

JESUS IN THE 'HOOD, JESUS IN THE 'BURBS

God posted the notices about the Messiah to the wrong addresses. He sent three astrologers chasing around Israel looking for a sign in the stars. He dispatched a raucous group of angels to the fields to inspire some dread and wonder among the local shepherd population. They were not the ideal people to start a worldwide movement.

Shepherds had always had a bit of a rough deal. David restored their image a little by writing about them in Psalm 23, but the fact that he had once been one indicated his status as the youngest in the family. Disputes over land gave the shepherds the kind of status often accorded to Native Indians or Gypsies. They were the victims of irrational prejudice, and to have the label was to be condemned. The religious authorities of the day had a list of occupations that were either unclean or borderline. Shepherds were among them.

The wise men came from another culture and possibly from a different religion, although they seemed familiar with the Old Testament. They were savvy enough to know that their dreams were from God and left without telling Herod what he wanted to know about the young Messiah's whereabouts.

God had also let the God chasers of that time know He was at work and alerted Simeon and Anna that Joseph and Mary had come to the temple to consecrate the baby Jesus. Simeon warned Mary and Joseph of the challenges they faced.

The arrival of the Christ was made known to every strata of society, including those deemed to belong to the less fortunate parts of it.

There is also a distinct lack of bias in Jesus friendship choices. Was He a man of the people? With several fishermen and Simon the Zealot among His disciples, He was in touch with the ordinary workingman. But He also had a tax collector, a middle class man, in the disciples' ranks.

How did Jesus get on with the elite of His day? Nicodemus, a member of the ruling council of the Jews, visited privately to talk.[20] Jesus also had friends among the rich, including Joseph of Arimathea, who purchased the place where He was briefly buried. Joseph was also a member of the Council and was prominent enough to be granted an audience with Pilate.[21]

Our vision of Jesus as the champion of the poor or the author of godly free enterprise will always need to be tempered by His unwillingness to conform to labels and neat categories. The hand that touched the leper, blessed the child, and washed the disciples feet was also extended to the rulers of His day.

Whenever a sectarian spirit might try to capture our mind, the obstinate paradoxes of an unprejudiced grace stand guard over our hearts.

Ask yourself, is there something about which I'm a bigot? Then ask yourself, what's my excuse? Then ponder this. Jesus was wronged at some point, by every section of society, but He kept on loving in a relentless fashion, aware of their imperfection, but believing the truth could set them free and restore them to their original purpose—loving God and loving their neighbor.

JESUS, IN THE WORLD BUT NOT OF IT

Because we read the Bible through faith-tinted glasses, we don't always read it slowly enough to see past the obvious and catch the meaningful detail. Jesus did a lot of very ordinary things amid the miracles, parables, and verbal dust ups with spiritually anxious teachers of the law.

He went out with some of the disciples while they did their work and actually helped them catch more fish than normal. He cooked breakfast for His disciples. He washed their feet. He visited people's homes a lot—even when it was not expedient in terms of his reputation, Zacchaeus the tax collector being a case in point. Even some of His miracles were very down to earth: Changing water into wine wouldn't be the first miracle of choice for the pentecostal-healer-in-training today. He made a social occasion more enjoyable!

At other times He had conversations that were likely to attract rebuke from everybody. He talked, while alone, to a woman who was immoral and a member of a despised group.[22]

Religious men were very wary about their contact with women they did not know. If they were menstruating, the man would be deemed to be ceremonially unclean for several days after their meeting, however innocent it might be. Jesus ignored this and risked contamination by letting the woman draw water for Him. He risked slurs on His reputation, given that the woman had been through five husbands and was living with someone she hadn't yet married.

Jesus expanded the boundaries of grace by sharing His life with her and other Samaritans who flocked to hear what He had to say.

Our initial reading of this story might focus on Jesus' insight into the woman's life and His extension of the Gospel to the Samaritans. If we only dwell there, we miss what to us is mundane. The holy teacher talked to a woman—not mundane in Jesus' day. The teacher asked the woman to give Him water, another physical threat to His spiritual integrity and an undermining, in the eyes of the purity obsessed teachers of the law, of Jesus' claim to be the Messiah, the Son of God. In their eyes, a real holy man would know that God would deliver a pure and holy nation and would not have risked His reputation.

It will be clear, as this book continues to unfold, that Jesus was not "of the world." He had not embraced its way of thinking. But His life is a severe provocation to those who would ask us to contain our lives in a Christian enclave, protected from this world and cut off from the mundane contact with people that allows communication, signals acceptance, and is sometimes countercultural because it crosses boundaries of class, gender, race, and creed.

Jesus didn't send His followers out alone. From the nurture of a strong community, they went out in twos to taint the world with goodness, looking out for each other in every circumstance of life.

Ask yourself these questions: Do I spend time with my neighbors or work colleagues or friends doing mundane, ordinary things? Do I eat with them, talk to them about sports, discuss the nature of our work, reflect on the news together? Do I believe that from their growing trust will flow the chance to talk about Jesus, life, and eternity, maybe next week, maybe next year?

Or is the reality that we are all prone to measure our time with people according to a guilt-related yardstick? "How can I share my faith? I must be careful to avoid talking about unspiritual things."

In Britain we have a social phenomena related to quiz nights. My wife and I are going regularly to one with a couple we have known for nearly twenty years. They're avowed agnostics. At the moment, they're grieving the loss of a close friend and need the comfort of uncomplicated friendship. We often talk of faith in passing—their son is involved at our church—but some nights we don't. It never occurs to me feel guilty when we don't talk about

Jesus, nor to feel that somehow my faith will be undermined by this friendship. It does occur to me that Jesus loves them and that I should love them too. It also occurs to me that He who is in us is greater than he that is in the world.[23]

Jesus asked the disciples to do very mundane things when they went out to the towns around Jerusalem. They were to greet people, eat with them, and then offer to pray for their healing before declaring to them that they were being invited to be part of a kingdom with a new set of values.[24]

Are you ready to be ordinary so the extraordinary can be seen in your life as the Holy Spirit prompts you?

AND THAT'S NOT ALL

We will return to the tension of Jesus' life again as you read on. Was Jesus pessimistic and optimistic? How did He use the Scripture and listen to the Spirit? What did His disciples learn in the everyday conversations and through the crisis times?

Living with the paradoxes in the life of Jesus doesn't involve compromise. You're not being asked to ignore parts of it. You are being asked to take it all seriously. It won't always be understood when you do.

Earlier in this chapter we remarked that John was accused of being demonized because He led an ascetic lifestyle. Jesus was called a glutton and drunkard because He celebrated the good gifts of His Father with people.

You'll find the same if you stand in God's center, embracing grace and justice, the rich and the poor, the pastoral and the prophetic, tradition and innovation.

But that's the challenge of following Jesus.

1. Philippians 2:6-11
2. Matthew 3:17
3. John 6:16-24
4. Luke 8:22-25
5. Luke 10:25-28
6. Matthew 5:17
7. Matthew 12:11
8. Mark 2:27, 3:4
9. 1 Corinthians 11:2, 11:23, 15:3
10. Luke 4:18-19
11. John 8: 10-12
12. Matthew 19:14; Mark 10:14; Luke 18:16
13. Mark 8:1-8
14. Luke 9:23
15. Luke 10:36-37, 13:31-32
16. Luke 11:29
17. Luke 19:41; John 11:35
18. Matthew 9:36, 20:34; Mark 1:41
19. Matthew 22:17
20. John 3:1-21
21. Mark 15:43
22. John 4:1-26
23. 1 John 4:4
24. Luke 10:5-9

4

A LONG OBEDIENCE

"Just As I Am" echoed around the 15,000-seat auditorium at a Billy Graham crusade, as an unbelieving eleven-year-old rose from his seat and strode toward the front. I was getting "saved" again.

Of course what you've just read is theologically questionable. I had committed my life to Christ at five. My decision at a Billy Graham crusade represented a more grown up me saying, "I still believe." At eighteen I would walk the aisle again seeking assurance and an empowering of the Holy Spirit.

At twenty-five I would sit on a train and read of the grace of God, given for me through Jesus, not capable of being earned, a work of God in His mercy and love. You need to understand at this point that I had felt for many years that I was a miserable failure. I remained drawn to Jesus, but I harbored the thought that feeling miserable for another thirty to forty years was not a thrilling prospect.

The Dyanmics of Spiritual Renewal had been recommended to me.[1] A minister admonished me to read chapter seven. As I sat on that train and began to read, I met with God long before that.

The author, Richard Lovelace, talked of a "naked reliance on the work of Christ" and a willingness to believe that "you are accepted." Like many, I had been looking for assurance, hoping that my sincerity would count for something, reminding myself that I was not a particularly bad person. My faith was looking for evidence of a God connection in all the wrong places. The place where it was to be found was in the character of God.

God loved me. He had sent His Son to introduce the values of the kingdom. His Son, Jesus, would then take the punishment that mankind's rebellion deserved as He suffered on the Cross. His resurrection would be God's thunderous "Yes" to the work of the Son and signal the beginning of the end for the devil and all those captivated by his evil designs.

I stepped off the train a changed man. Walking home, I resolved to discover more about the character of God and the work of Jesus, believing that this would be key in helping me move from being a miserable worrier to a joyful servant of God. I needed to move from a mental conversation with God that was marked by the nagging question: "Am I alright?" to one which said, "Thanks, I'm grateful, You are good."

For so long I had thought that pleasing God meant an avoidance of sin. Now it began to dawn on me that I could spend the rest of my life seeking to manage my sin and despising myself, or I could start to embark on a journey toward joy in the service of God.

That journey would explore the salvation story and form values and choices which would lead me toward a life resonating with the character of God. I would be obedient because I understood something of the heart of God and was beginning to comprehend the wisdom of the boundaries He suggested.

I would actually view sin or rebellion against God with a greater seriousness as a result. But there was a difference. My individual view of my sin and my relationship with a holy God before would always drive me inward and toward rules, laws, and formulas. Stepping back and seeing that God had a purpose for me within the community of believers and within the wider community drew me out of my scrutiny of my spiritual standing and toward expressing my faith in the everyday rhythms of life.

I became captivated by the idea that Jesus was a liberator. When I was preaching and I touched on this, something would happen to me. I couldn't stand still. I would pace the platform, trying to articulate this feeling of release, joy, deliverance, purpose, and vision that would sweep over me.

"Why should holiness be miserable?" I would exalt. "Isn't seeing people healed, restored and forgiven a joyful thing? Isn't seeing families reconciled a joyful thing? Isn't seeing the awkward, rejected person finding a place of security and acceptance joyful?" Sometimes I could hardly speak. I wanted people to know the truth and for the truth to set them free.

But something still nagged me. How did we grow in faith? What helped us become spiritually mature? How could we avoid abusing God's grace by continuing in sinful patterns of behavior?

As the years progressed, I began a two-track journey of discovery. I began to be aware of what I believe were half answers—truthful answers if they were part of a larger story, but a poison if they weren't.

I also had one of those moments which change the way you think without you even realizing it at the time. I was staging seminars for youth leaders on contemporary culture. I wanted some snappy titles to give to the program. I simply wrote "Seven Ways that Culture Shapes Young People." Books that gave seven-part formulas were very popular at the time.

I then sat down to ensure that I had seven main points I could make. Part of me wishes I could yell you that I received a profound insight via a mystical experience. The reality was that I discovered a framework that helped me, because I needed to meet the promise of my seminar title. But first let's look at the half answers.

HALF ANSWERS

Helping people grow spiritually can be a minefield. This partly relates to the fact that we can turn what works for us into an absolute. As far as we're concerned, it's the best way. We see the weakness of other ways, but we're not ready to admit the weakness of ours.

It seems to me that the Scripture suggests to us principle of combination. These combinations bring health, but each element on its own only has a very small contribution.

Take for instance the oil of anointing. This was used in the Old Testament and contained olive oil, myrrh, cinnamon, calamus, and cassia. Together these elements made fragrant oil that warmed your skin when it was poured on you. God ordained specific quantities and elements for inclusion.[2] Each element was said to be symbolic of something—cassia of humility, myrrh of sacrifice, cinnamon of holiness, and calamus of the cost of redemption. Olive oil was associated with righteousness and fruitfulness.

The pattern occurred again in the New Testament when the Apostle described the nature of the church in Ephesians 4:11: "It was he who gave some to be apostles, some to be prophets, some to be evangelicals and some to be pastors and teachers, to prepare God's people for works of service."

The idea that a combination works best is echoed in the biblical metaphor of the body: "As it is, there are many parts, but one body …. Those parts of the body that seem weaker are indispensable."[3]

Paul asked rhetorically, "Are all apostles, are all prophets." The Church and the individuals within it seem to need a diverse foundation on which to establish their spiritual building.

The reality is that while combinations of spiritual nurture may be the biblical pattern, we can sometimes become infatuated with one "technology" that we consider our spiritual "killer app." Here are a few to jog your memory.

GUILT

Even the most saintly, focused, purposeful Christian will sometimes experience temptation and may even stumble. A call to holiness, purity, and right living may at times be a vital part of our church life.

Then again, guilt can be used like a pepper spray. It'll make you cry. It'll make you stop for a while, but will it change your mind? It's all too easy for us to speak the words: "Today sin is walking the corridors of this church; God wants to come and clean house." It may be true, but when we speak it out week after week, it actually suggests several things. The preacher may have an ego that needs to see response. The church board may want tangible results, and regular guilt trips produce apparent responses.

But if we are only the travel agents for guilt trips, the congregation may hear a more subtle and devastating message. "This isn't working. People ask for prayer every week, so why aren't they growing up?"

Guilt can be godly, particularly when it relates to real objective sin events, but I think of it as a handbrake. It helps you stop sinning, but it doesn't help you steer. The values of the kingdom of God are the steering wheel of the Christian bus.

Is the dirge of guilt the only tune sung in your church?

EXPERIENCE

Some of us live in a shadow world of doubt and faith. We can't shake the lingering feeling that God is real, Jesus is Prince of Peace, and the Holy Spirit is our comforter, but actually we wonder if it's true at all.

We hanker after validating experiences, moments of high spiritual drama which make it all seem more real. We talk of "meeting with God" and "needing to feel His touch" on our lives.

None of this is wrong. Peter's dream on the roof that kickstarted the mission to the gentiles, Jesus' joust with Satan in the desert, Paul's physically draining confrontation with the risen Christ on the road to Damascus: These were all tangible experiences.

But it can be wrong. It becomes a bargaining match with God. "I'll follow you if you can give me an experience." "I'll stop sinning if you release a powerful anointing of the Holy Spirit on me." It's a lazy person's path to personal holiness. "Show me You're there and turn me into an obedient robot."

It's not God's way. It's like someone playing the lead violin sheet music but there being no orchestra. It might sound okay, but it's missing the lushness that the rest of the orchestra brings.

EXAMPLE
We're encouraged by the Apostle Paul to be Christ-like, and we will often find that others in our church and community can model grace, mercy, and compassion to us.[4]

But if we're not careful, we can slip into feelings of spiritual inadequacy because we are not like our pastors, elders, or deacons. We can become disappointed when we discover that whatever their virtues, they are frail human beings with weaknesses and failings.

We may find ourselves traveling the road to the town of disappointment. Why doesn't God help me be like them? Why aren't they perfect? Perhaps I'm just useless? If we're not careful, we become disappointed when we're not like someone we admire. We end up coveting their gift rather than simply valuing it and trusting that God will use us according to our gifts.

There is a temptation toward idolatry lurking in our lives. We can end up infatuated with the methods of spiritual growth, rather than the creator who gave it to us, obsessed with the technology of discipleship rather than the disciple maker.

There are multiple factors at work in our spiritual growth. We should beware of isolating any one method as the only answer— let me outline the seven learning paths I uncovered as I sought to make sense of how culture shaped young people's minds.

The initial temptation for my audience and myself was to regard these paths as the property of our adversary the devil, but actually they are God's paths and the way He reveals truth to each new generation. They can carry thoughts and worldviews that speak of the glory of God, or they can be the carriers of rebellion and destruction.

How did God anticipate we might learn of Him? Here is a summary of what we will explore in the chapters that follow. I have seven distinct ideas, but I'm reading a book at the moment that has twelve. These seven are not meant be the definitive word, but they are the ones I've explored so far.

ROOTS—GOD'S ACTION IN HISTORY

God was known by His words expressed through the writers of the Hebrew Scripture, by the words of the prophets, and by His interventions into history.

This was expressed in the songs of the people and most particularly in the Psalms. Psalm 136 recounts the creation, the deliverance of God's people from oppression in Egypt, their life under various kings, and God's specific provision for individuals. Psalm 106 goes into even greater detail, warning the listener of the consequences of various rebellions, including the worship of the golden calf.

It's worth noting that there was a relentless common sense attitude about the Hebrews. The boat in their story of the flood was capable of doing all that the story claimed in terms of accommodating animals. Some millennia later, the early disciples were not content to claim Jesus was of the House of David; they backed it up with a detailed family tree (Matthew 1:1-17).

Jesus deliberately placed Himself within the prophetic tradition of Israel with one of His earliest statements. He shattered the calm of an ordinary Sabbath in the synagogue by announcing:

The spirit of the Lord is upon me.
Because he has anointed me
To preach good news to the poor
He has sent to proclaim the freedom for the prisoners
And recovery of sight for the blind
To release the oppressed
To proclaim the year of the Lord's favor.

He paused, returned the scroll to the attendant, sat down, and as every eye remained on him He said, "Today this scripture is fulfilled in your hearing."[5]

Jesus was keenly aware of His roots. He hadn't come to demolish the Old traditions or reject the salvation history story that had unfolded in the Old Testament. He had come to fulfill its promise.

How will our understanding of our roots shape how we follow Jesus? What can we learn from the past? Who has wrestled with some of the issues we face today? We'll explore these questions in chapter eight, "An Ancient and Future Faith."

Suffice it to say this: There is nothing new under the sun. What has been will be again.[6] If we are not aware of our past, we will neither understand the present nor be able to navigate the future.

LEARNING BY DOING

Church culture can be a very passive experience if we are not careful. Our minds are captivated by the idea that if we have powerful pulpit preaching in our church, then the congregation will be healthy and the Church will flourish.

For a significant number of people who have a temperamental disposition toward analysis, the forty-minute sermon may be very helpful. They go away and process the information and act on it. Many do not engage with it all. Their spiritual nurture may come through personal conversation, biblical reading, prayer, and Christian literature.

Most of us will also learn by doing. It was a keynote of the training of the twelve disciples and others who followed Jesus. In chapter seven, "Swimming Lessons with St. Peter," we will examine this possibility and reflect on what it demands of us.

The disciples heard several months of Jesus' teaching. He then sent them out with very simple instructions. Greet people, eat with them, pray for them, tell them the kingdom is near. They were to be in His advance party, encountering some problems they knew how to pray about and some they had to come back and seek further advice about. Learning by doing involves risk—risk on the part of the wise mentor and risk on the part of the disciple.

Can you handle the risk of following Jesus?

PARABLE
The story is told of two rabbis who came to a village. One was a master teacher of the law and could guide people through the complexity of ceremony, ritual, and purity. The other was a simple storyteller.

After some time, the villagers began to vote with their feet and kept returning to the storytelling rabbi to hear his wisdom.

The learned-in-the-law rabbi, the more senior of the two, was annoyed and spoke sharply to the storyteller, lamenting the people's attraction to the less demanding rhythms of the stories.

The storyteller turned to him and asked who the people of the village might go to if two traders approached them, one carrying diamonds, the other, small, clay kitchen vessels.

Little more needed to be said. The value of the learned rabbi's insights were affirmed as being rich and of great value, but the storyteller's stories were, like the clay pots, immediately useful and affordable for the ordinary people.

Jesus combined the styles of both rabbis. In his conversation with Nicodemus, He discusses concepts and principles with a man who was a leading religious figure of the day.[7] But He often used poetic forms, the Sermon on the Mount being one example, and parable/proverb when speaking with the ordinary man and woman.

He met them where they were and, as we will discover in chapter 6, "Once upon a Time," skillfully communicated the values of His new kingdom in a way that painted pictures on the minds of His listeners and touched their hearts with the emotions of grace, forgiveness, justice, and the compassion of God the Father.

A postmodern generation may cast doubt on the history of salvation through Jesus as the narrative that will guide them, but they are still captivated by stories and will often use them as the place to start in reflecting on culture and life. From soap operas to *West Wing*, from *Sex in the City* to *Law and Order*, from *Toy Story* to *Finding Nemo*, the story both reflects and captivates.

Think for a moment of the animated film *Shrek*. The story of two mythic creatures who remain in love even after it's clear that neither is conventionally beautiful, despite how they initially appeared, was a powerful comment on a physique obsessed generation and was the courier of a philosophical point that was as profound as the film was funny.

Are you a storyteller? Or do you simply quote texts? Following Jesus will mean doing both.

TRADITION

Those who worship spontaneously have no time for tradition. They thirst for the modern, the new, the contemporary, the cutting edge. They're often like the people of Israel, circling the desert waiting to enter the Promised Land. They know their God is there somewhere, but they're not sure how to get there. They have exciting times, and new theories sustain their energy while they wait for breakthrough, but often they're simple putty in the hands of a dominant personality who uses the spontaneous utterance to promote his own agenda.

Those who worship tradition on the other hand are sometimes locked into an idolatry of the ritual or established practice, rather than being captivated by the truth that lies behind it.

"Don't change a thing" sings one choir; "Change everything," responds the other.

Jesus wouldn't sing with either choir. He was a both/and person. He practiced the everyday traditions and the ancient practices of Israel, but ignored secondary rules put in place by spiritual bureaucrats. He celebrated the Passover and visited the temple to pray—these were His kind of traditions. He healed on the Sabbath and touched the unclean despite the irritation this sparked among the teachers of the law—compassion and mercy were more important than the myriad of rules with which the teachers of the law had obscured the principles of the Old Testament.

Tradition had its place in His life, and He used it to create theaters of memory and imagination, adding a new dimension to the Passover meal by using bread to symbolize His body and wine to symbolize His blood.

Tradition, as we will discover in chapter nine, "Give Me That Very Old Time Religion," was not meant to be the mere repeating of formulas and creeds, laden with a sense of obligation, but an intentional commitment to remember the work of God.

Tradition drew you back into the story that shaped your views of life.

HEROES

As he ran around our garden, my youngest son attempted to execute a Cruyff turn. This was a fluid dribbling movement artfully executed by the famous Dutch soccer player Johan Cruyff, now an object of wonder to legions of young players. He also wrestled with the Maradonna flick, which involves a more complicated foot and heel movement that causes the ball to rise vertically and achieves very little except pleasing the crowd. My son wanted to emulate the masters of the craft.

As I began to write in my late twenties, I was influenced by the unconventional writing of Tom Wolfe (Bonfire of the Vanities), a fluid conversational style that cared little for the normal rules of grammar, but conveyed emotion powerfully.

We all have heroes. We study their craft, we note their character, and we absorb their insights. They are objects of awe and also of inspiration. Jesus had an example. He only did what He saw the Father doing.[8] Paul calls us to follow his example as he follows Christ's.[9]

Those who are our examples make the theories tangible; they make the challenges seem possible. They release hope and inspire us to persevere; they make our faith seem plausible. In "Heroes of the Faith," chapter nine, we'll look at how the life of another can shape ours and how answers march out from the pages of the Bible and history to help us live for Jesus today.

REVELATION

God uses both the natural and the supernatural to help us discover more about Him. Many churches major on revelation, at the expense of the other learning paths that we have mentioned. We can react against that but in seeking to ensure that we embrace all of God's means and methods, we will not want to neglect the basic building block of our faith.

NATURAL REVELATION

Psalm 19 tells us the "heavens declare the glory of God; the skies proclaim the work of his hands. Day after day they pour forth speech … There is no speech or language where their voice is not heard."

THE WORD OF GOD

The Bible is our record of the work of God through the millennia. As we read it we feed both the mind and the spirit. We quip ourselves with facts and frameworks of thought. We will also find it challenging us and provoking us to both reflection and action. The Holy Spirit interacts with us as we read it and brings it alive to us.

PRAYER

In prayer we enter into a two-way conversation. God will speak to us as much as we speak to Him—if we will listen.

COMMUNITY

God has placed us in families and communities of faith so that we can learn from one another. The Scripture encourages us to not "neglect meeting together," because church is an event through which we can receive revelation and insight into the character of God and the work of Christ.[10]

In Chapter 11, "Habits of the Heart," we examine in more depth the possibilities for us all as we seek to be receivers of revelation.

LIFE EXPERIENCE

There are some things that simply happen in your life. You can't make intentional decisions to explore them. You can't attend courses to discover them. They simply happen.

I once sat on a train, reading the story of the infamous bassist, Sid Vicious, a member of the pioneering punk band The Sex Pistols. The story was told from the perspective of his girlfriend's mother.

The moment when the mother discovers in the hallways of her suburban home that her troubled daughter has died in violent circumstances is a confusion of emotions: sorrow at the loss of her daughter; anger at the pain of the previous five years; relief that it was finally over.

It took every ounce of my personal self-control to not break down and cry out loud. The emotion was a surprise. I was not a habitual weeper. I felt like I was feeling the emotions of the mother. My heart had been moved in a situation that was in no way premeditated. I had met the God of surprises.

It was to be a moment of revelation for me. Raised in a Christian home in a situation of relative security, I tended to view other people's emotions with a clinical detachment. Sin and its consequences in causing human misery were a theological concept to me rather than something I could really empathize with, understand, or offer a constructive response to.

Sitting in that crowded commuter train as it sped into London, something prideful and judgmental was broken in me. I became at once more serious about sin and more sympathetic to those caught and captivated by it. My heart was softer and my mind more militant.

God had spoken through the brokenness of another in order to help me follow Jesus. Sometimes you hear His voice when you feel that there is a part of your life you would rather forget about.

I spent two years trying to help a former drug dealer grow in faith. He was abusive and manipulative, but could appear deeply "spiritual" when he wanted to. I would close and stand in front doors so he couldn't run out when confronted about his outspoken attacks on individuals in public or his disturbing verbal attacks on his wife.

I would be assaulted by doubt over my handling of him, even after he had sworn at me in public places or lied to me with no sign of remorse. He seduced a woman in our church and eventually left town to a sigh of collective relief among the local churches.

I felt like a failure, but the lessons I had absorbed as I cried on a train were now more concrete. I had seen the crestfallen anguish and hurt cross someone's face when they were verbally abused. When this man degraded his wife, I fought the urge to give him the right fist of fellowship. I had contained my own mirth when one of my sons, unschooled in spiritual etiquette at the age of four, had given him a sharp blow in the groin as he shouted at me. It was followed by a warning to not shout out at me again, as the angry man recovered from this attack on his manhood.

Sin as habit or a direction of heart was becoming less academic to me. I had always been aware of my own shortcomings but unaware of the pain others carried. I had witnessed it firsthand.

It released a holy desperation. I had to know how people grew in faith. I had to understand how I could help others be more like Christ. I had learned from my life experiences and continue to do so to this day.

Following Jesus. Are you willing to orientate your life around some simple but profound ideas?

- We learn from the fathers of our faith.
- We learn from the Holy Spirit as He speaks via prayer, Scripture, nature, and personal impression.
- We learn by doing.
- We learn from stories, proverbs, and word pictures.
- We learn from the traditions that shape our worship and our lives together.
- We learn from the example of others.
- We learn from the events of our lives, both good and bad.

Think of following Jesus as being like constructing a jigsaw puzzle. The Bible is your guide picture. The jigsaw is your life. Be patient with yourself as you put the picture together.

It takes a long obedience.

1. Richard Lovelace, *The Dynamics of Spiritual Renewal* (Paternoster Press).
2. Exodus 30:22-33
3. 1 Corinthians 12:20-31
4. 1 Corinthians 11:1; 1 Timothy 4:12
5. Luke 4:18-20; Isaiah 61:1-2
6. Ecclesiastes 1:9
7. John 3:1-21
8. John 5:19
9. 1 Corinthians 11:1
10. Hebrews 10:25

5

A MESSAGE FROM OUR SPONSOR

I was in a hostile environment. It was a religious arts festival, where I was defending the idea that Jesus was the only way to God. An audience of astonishing spiritual diversity was not hesitating to tell me how wrong I was.

I had the audacity to suggest that much of the reasoning I was hearing was based on sentiment, and that it could not appeal to any authority beyond the feelings of the one declaring it. "If all roads lead to God," I enquired, "on what basis would you exclude the Christian identity racists, the Wahhabi and Deobondi extremists that have helped create the Taliban and Al Qaeda and the German pagan religions that fostered the brutal terrors of Adolf Hitler and National Socialism?"

I emerged cheerful and unscathed from this encounter with the debating classes of liberal Christianity. One thing was clear, however. They weren't looking to the Bible as a standard against which to weigh their theories.

The challenge for you and I as we seek to follow Jesus is to understand how we are to view the Bible and how we might read it and use it as part of our desire to be disciples.

Paul reminds Timothy that the Scripture is "God-breathed" and is useful for teaching, correction, and training. If we are to fully understand what this means for us, we need to answer three questions:

How did Jesus use the Old Testament Scripture? How exhaustive is the guidance we are given in Scripture? How are we to interpret the Scripture?

Jesus was intimately acquainted with the Old Testament and used it frequently to illustrate His points and respond to teachers of the law.

THE TORAH

This refers to the first five books, from Genesis to Deuteronomy. It contains the story of the origins of mankind and the religious framework of teaching that helped guide the Israelite nation. It contained advice on how to conduct their festivals and the ethical foundations of The Ten Commandments, as well as sundry other advice about agriculture, conduct in war, personal hygiene, dietary advice, and advice on keeping the genetics of the tribe from getting too chaotic.

Jesus refers to the Torah throughout His ministry, but quite specifically uses it during His encounter with the devil in the wilderness. "Man does not live by bread alone. Do not put the Lord your God to the test. Worship the Lord your God and serve Him only." These were His three responses to the taunting, mocking, and bribery of the evil one and are drawn from the book of Deuteronomy.[1]

God's purpose in Creation, His framework for living a life of wholeness and peaceful "shalom," and His desire to help mankind reject that which destroys them are all found in the Torah and are echoed in the life of Jesus.

HISTORICAL BOOKS

These include all the books from Judges to Esther and particularly cover the period when David was king. Jesus does not specifically refer to these books, but the New Testament affirms Jesus as having come from the family line of David because of the lineage of his mother Mary.[2] Jesus also references the Psalms, many of which were written by David during this period. Much of what we learn in these books concerns the fruit of man's pride and rebellion as kings and priests set aside the wisdom of God to pursue their own ways. These lead them into captivity and exile and created the situation where God must become man through Jesus and show us the reality of what God desires.

THE POETIC BOOKS

These include Job through Song of Songs. They are a diverse group of books. One is an epic about one man's suffering (Job), another the Bible's most erotic book (Song of Songs). Proverbs is a vast collection of pithy sayings; Ecclesiastes a lament. The book of Psalms is a songbook and appears often in the story of Jesus.

Satan tempts Him with a reminder that God could protect Jesus if He threw Himself off a tower.[3] Those welcoming His arrival into Jerusalem quote Psalm 118 as they chant: "Blessed is he who comes in the name of the Lord." Jesus refers to the fact that God has ordained praise from the mouth of infants as a response to those criticizing this demonstration of regard for the Messiah.

The poetic wisdom books remind us of several things. They have an emotional honesty which is captured by the lament in Psalm 13:

How long must I wrestle with my thoughts
and every day have sorrow in my heart?
How long will my enemy triumph over me?

But I trust in your unfailing love;
my heart rejoices in your salvation.
I will sing to the LORD,
for he has been good to me.

They resonate with the magnificent imagery of nature and

creation as the writers declare in terms that the mind can grasp the magnificence of God.

He wraps himself in light as with a garment; he stretches out the heavens like a tent (Psalm 104:2).

These richly textured books give us permission to make songs, poetry, and laments that reflect our commitment to the Creator.

THE PROPHETS

Jesus is identified in the Gospels as a reflection of the prophetic tradition of Isaiah. His birth is foretold by the prophet who speaks of a wonderful counselor and Prince of Peace who will some day come. In the climatic moment of confrontation with the money changers in the temple, Jesus refers to the words of Isaiah who said the temple would be a house of prayer.[4]

Speaking of the end of days, Jesus refers also to the apocalyptic visions of Daniel and the "abomination that causes desolation."[5]

Jesus also appealed to the prophetic tradition. He reminds the pharisees that God desires mercy more than sacrifice on two occasions.[6] He deliberately identifies with the justice tradition of the prophets when He rises in the synagogue and says:

The Spirit of the Lord is on me,
because he has anointed me
to preach good news to the poor.
He has sent me to proclaim freedom for the prisoners
and recovery of sight for the blind,
to release the oppressed,
to proclaim the year of the Lord's favor.
(Luke 4:18-19, Isaiah 61:1-2)

Those who exploit the poor are robbing them of their God-given dignity, treating them as something less than image-bearers of God.

BUT WHAT DOES IT MEAN?

The epistles reflect the teaching given to or approved by those who were "eye-witnesses" of His majesty and further expand our understanding of the life, work, and ministry of Jesus.[7]

Our approach to the Bible is therefore Christ-centered, deriving its authority from His affirmation of the Old Testament, the story of His life, and the influence of those who walked the earth with Him. It is much more than a helpful story. It contains the wisdom that can help us make sense of creation, our lives, and the future. It's God's Word to us.

In seeking to understand the life of Jesus and what He desires of us as His followers, we look for the "main and plain" meaning of the words in front of us. The Apostle Paul worried about those who claim secret knowledge, work out endless genealogies, and distort the truth with teachings from other religions.[8] The belief in numerology that undergirds the idea of the Bible Code or the speculation that sometimes arises about the exact date of Christ's return would fall into Paul's category of issues that cause division.

Your church may have introduced you to the tools of understanding you need. If it hasn't, you may want to help yourself understand the Bible and the life of Christ by remembering the grammar and history test. What is the simple, direct, plain, ordinary, and literal sense of the phrases, clauses, and sentences you are reading?

If you then seek out books and commentaries that carefully consider the time and circumstances in which the author wrote, you will be able to paint in the extra detail that will help you make sense of the story. As you read on in this book, you will note that I do this quite often with respect to the words and deeds of Jesus.

When you discover the status of the tax collectors, then Jesus' actions take on a different meaning. We can understand that people don't like tax collectors. People in our culture don't either. We can understand that people might be hostile to those who helped out an occupying force. When we become aware that there were seven professions that were considered automatically unclean and that this included tax collectors, then Jesus' attitude to them becomes more than an act of kindness.

It's an act of spiritual sedition. He spent an afternoon with Matthew and tax collecting friends and upset the whole city of Jericho by going to the home of Zacchaeus.

The grammatical historical method is wary of the idea that a passage might have multiple meanings. Remember main and plain.

TEXT BOOK OR TEST BOOK

The Bible is however not always exhaustive in what its says. We should regard it as a test book rather than a textbook. It often infers rather than spells out in detail. Here are some examples.

WORSHIP

Some denominations suggest that because instrumental music is not mentioned in the New Testament (NT), then our worship should be the same as the NT, as the NT is a more complete picture of God's will than the Old Testament (OT). The weakness of this is that it undermines the essential unity of scripture and doesn't do justice to verses that reference the psalms as a model for worship alongside hymns and spiritual songs.[9] Seems to me you can't sing about praising the Lord with dance, tambourine, harp, and lyre without feeling that perhaps you should take the words seriously.[10]

MARRIAGE

Elders have to be the husband of one wife. Jesus forbids divorce except in the case of adultery. Paul warns about fornication. Jesus tells stories about virgins at a wedding feast who have failed to ensure they have enough oil for their lamps. The Church is compared to a bride. What's missing from this picture? An actual description of what a wedding ceremony might contain. We infer that a ceremony where covenant promises are made would be good, but the details are not spelled out for us.

The Bible affirms much but doesn't always fill in the ceremonial or practical detail. Sometimes we have to look for the underlying principles.

WHAT'S THE PATTERN?

We have to look for the patterns because verses or passages on their own don't tell us the whole story. Sometimes we can take a verse and build the picture around it. Take for instance:

Therefore go and make disciples of all nations, baptizing them in the name of the Father and of the Son and of the Holy Spirit (Matthew 28:19).

This is the only verse in Scripture where all three aspects of the godhead are mentioned in the same sentence. The Gospels tell us of Jesus and remind us that Isaiah promised that He would come.[11] His death is foreshadowed in Psalm 22, which speaks of a forsaken man who is mocked by those who say He should rescue Himself.[12] The revelation of God in the Old Testament already contains the promise of the Son. Jesus in turn tells the disciples that if they have seen Him, they have seen the Father.[13] He also promises to leave the Holy Spirit with them as a counselor. This same Holy Spirit has been with Him throughout His ministry and led Him into the desert to fast and pray before the period of His public ministry began.[14]

We infer our doctrine of the Trinity, the mystery of how God is both one and three, from these and many other passages.

LET'S GET ETHICAL

Sometimes the pattern is not even explicit in Scripture, but it is our job to connect our Scripture-prompted goals with the realities of life.

To help ensure that social chaos did not arise as a result of sexual immorality, God encouraged the idea of marriage. There was provision for divorce, and Jesus strengthened this so that it would only include adultery as grounds for separation and dissolving the marriage. The stability of a committed relationship helped ensure financial stability, property and land ownership stability, emotional security, and a protecting atmosphere for growing children.

Anything which undermines this faithfulness and commitment is viewed with prejudice in the Scripture. The adulterous woman who would entrap the gullible is a key figure in the book of Proverbs. The sexual acquisitiveness of King David was to be his downfall, as his affair with Bathsheba unraveled into murder and deceit. It was to cost him the ambition of his life, namely the building of the temple. Paul is keen that couples keep each other happy in bed and warns them only to abstain by mutual consent and for the purpose of prayer.

There is a pattern of encouragement and warnings that have one goal in mind: the preservation of the family unit. Self-control is to be aided by this wider commitment to God's purposes expressed in the covenant of marriage.

With this in mind, we approach the wider issues of sexuality and particularly masturbation and pornography. The Church has traditionally warned of the dangers of masturbation, with voices lost in history but not popular mythology, suggesting that it made you go blind, mad, or both. The reality, however, is that there is no explicit biblical injunction against it.

The Bible does refer, however to Onan spilling his "seed" on the ground.[15] This is, however a reference to his unwillingness to honor the traditional commitment that a brother would make to marry his sister-in-law should she become a widow, and it was his refusal to honor this and fulfill his marital commitment that angered God.

Not masturbating then becomes an issue of avoiding behavior that will make it difficult to maintain sexual self-control before marriage and avoid adultery within it. Pornography creates an expectation that may not be possible to fulfill within a marriage, and also promotes the lie of the desirable image against which some spouses may not measure up.

Pornography and masturbation can be a form of adultery, where the coveting of another person's body leads to actual sin.

Christian teaching in this area can appeal to the big picture of biblical wisdom and suggest that an avoidance of masturbation is helpful. It can't, however, appeal to a chapter and verse biblical denunciation.

Interpreting Scripture is the stuff of many books, but the underlying principles that inform my vision of what it means to follow Jesus are these:

We should seek:

- The main and plain meaning of Scripture. We can understand truth in the light of what we can learn from the history of our time.
- We can use the Scripture to test our practices, but the Bible is not an exhaustive textbook.
- We need to look for explicit patterns in the Scripture that help us understand the broad sweep of God's revelation.
- Some of our discipleship decisions will be a response to a biblical ethical principle, rather than something the Bible explicitly mentions.

If you're following Jesus, you have to do it by the book!

1. Deuteronomy 8:3; 6:13,16
2. Matthew 1:16
3. Psalm 91:11-12; Matthew 4:6
4. Isaiah 56:7
5. Matthew 24:15; Daniel 9:27
6. Hosea 6:6

7. Luke 1:2; 2 Peter 1:16
8. 1 Timothy 1:4; Titus 3:9
9. Ephesians 5:19; Colossians 3:16
10. Psalm 149, 150
11. Matthew 1:23; Isaiah 7:14
12. Matthew 27:43
13. John 14:7-10
14. John 14:26; Mark 1:12
15. Genesis 38:9

6

ONCE UPON A TIME

Jesus was drawing in the sand. All around Him was an irate and emotionally charged crowd. Some were fearful. His disciples must have been wondering how Jesus was going to handle the taunting question thrown at Him.

"Moses told us to stone such women. Now what do you say?"[1]

Others were scheming, hoping that their question would undermine the teacher whose popularity threatened the status quo. Perhaps the rest were simply there to witness the spectacle of death or bloodshed.

What was Jesus to do? He couldn't agree with the woman's adulterous lifestyle. He would be wary of undermining the Old Testament revelation that He quoted so often.

In the event, He warned them of their own vulnerability to sin and rebellion, and they slipped away, guilty, and deflated.

Jesus was a powerful communicator, using proverbs, parables, and symbolic action. Even His body language, reflected in this case by an apparently unconcerned, unpressured drawing in the sand, may speak to us, although some commentators believe that He may have been averting His eyes from the woman's semi-nakedness.

ANCIENT METHODS/FUTURE CHURCH

Imagine for a moment you live in the culture of Jesus' day. World history doesn't arrive via digital signals to screens in your living room or study. Books are not generally available, and you can't listen to the audiocassettes of your favorite speaker.

How did Jesus communicate, and what do His ancient methods have to say to our future Church life? How did He pass on His values and equip twelve men to start a Church that would shape civilizations and attract billions of followers?

It's tempting to think it was because He was a great orator. He clearly was. He sat in a boat and, using the acoustic properties of the nearby coastline, spoke to thousands. He taught more than 4,000 people for three days on another occasion. But as you read the biblical record, you'll find few long speeches or lengthy sermons. The Sermon on the Mount narratives don't take much more than seven minutes to read out loud.

So He must have been doing something else. If we are to follow Jesus and create countercultural communities, we are clearly going to have to do more than ensure that our Sunday services are finished by an eloquent forty-minute sermon, useful as that may be.

There are seven learning paths for us to discover in the life of Jesus. They are all entirely relevant to the people of God today. In this chapter we'll deal with the first—the power of story.

JESUS THE STORYTELLER

Jesus once told the story of a son who demanded his inheritance, squandered it, and then returned to his father, contrite and ready to work as a servant.

The story elicits an emotional response from the listener, in a way that a mere statement would not. Imagine someone tells you God is a loving Father. It's a fine thought, but in its propositional form, it's merely a statement of belief.

But as Jesus unfolds the story of the prodigal son, the whole person of the listener is engaged. They hear the statements; they can visualize the situation in their mind's eye and may begin to experience the emotions of the various participants of the story. You learn a lesson about a word that is never mentioned: forgiveness.

Let's immerse ourselves in the story. The son's request for his share of the inheritance would be akin to wishing your father would die. The father nevertheless gives him what he requests. The mere fact that there was an inheritance to be divided suggests that the father of the story was an affluent man. We later discover he has servants and considerable livestock, jewels, and fine clothing. Imagine the impact on the local economy of his son taking a large amount of money to another city or place? What would local people feel about this son, who was quite possibly damaging the livelihood of the people in that community?

When the son has spent all his money, he finds his friendship circle is fickle, and he is now alone. Jesus' listeners were likely to have shuddered at the thought that he was reduced to feeding pigs, an unclean animal as far as the Jewish believer was concerned, although some may have felt he was reaping what he had sowed.

He decides to throw himself on the mercy of his family and offer to work, even as a servant. So far so good, and our theme of the rebellious son seeking forgiveness and mercy is developing nicely.

Jesus' description of the behavior of the father adds new emotional depth to the story, conveying this in small but poignant phrases: While the son was "still a long way off," the father saw him and "was filled with compassion for him." The father chooses mercy when he could have chosen anger or righteous indignation. Perhaps, however, we miss the visual symbolism of what happens next. The father runs to him, hitching up his robes, an unusual act for an older man in Israelite culture. He then embraces the son before the son speaks and kisses him. Even before his contrition is verbally expressed, the father signals acceptance to the son.

Jesus doesn't mention the local community, but would they have been in the mind of the listener? Some commentators believe that the father was running to the rescue of the son. Despite the hospitality of Middle Eastern communities, an elder or community leader could signal danger to a village by smashing a pot over the head of a hostile party or an unwanted visitor.

The wronged father comes to the rescue of his errant child and then lavishes on him the best he has. He arranges for his feet to be cleaned and shod, a ring to be placed on his finger, which signals his family restoration, and the robe usually reserved for visiting dignitaries to be placed around his shoulders. The best food is prepared, and a party begins. The lost son had been found; the one feared dead is alive.

Jesus then discusses the reaction of the brother, who basically asks why good gifts are being lavished on a bad son, when he has never even had a young goat to feast on. The father reminds him that all the property and riches he has will one day belong to the stay-at-home son, but encourages him to rejoice in the restoration of his brother.

FEELING THE STORY

Over the years different aspects of this story have had a strong resonance for me.

I sat one day in a traditional mainline church and heard in my heart, not merely in my head, the words "and while he was still a long way off." Perhaps you've experienced that almost detached stillness when a sentence really captures your attention. God was active in His desire to restore, waiting for us to turn our hearts toward home. I felt the emotion of one reminded of great love rising in me, a comparatively rare experience at the time.

Years later, I sat in my study reading a commentary on this story as I prepared to speak. It began to dawn on me that the father's haste to greet his son was not merely the reaction of a sentimental and forgiving father, but the father's active desire to rescue the son from possible danger.

In my mind's eye, I visualized myself preaching about the love of the rescuing Father and felt that urgency I often feel when talking about Jesus the liberator, the earthly expression of the God who gave of Himself to reconcile man to Him. There are moments when you almost want to compel people to discover the life, death, and resurrection of Jesus. You want to help them grasp the love of God and the wisdom that will restore their lives, heal their hurts, and give them direction for the future.

PICTURE THIS

The fable of the prodigal would have touched Jesus' listeners at many levels and continues to touch people today. Jesus used stories, word pictures, and metaphors to help His listeners understand, if they were open, the truth about God, life, and creation. He talked of pearls, sheep, unjust stewards, persistent neighbors, and wayward sons, ungrateful guests, and wise stewards.

Little was otherworldly in His speech; He left memorable word images behind as eternal reminders of the message He brought.

This wasn't unique to Jesus and was part of the creative impulse of the psalmist and the prophet.

Imagine for a moment you're in church. During one of the prayers, Brother Blessed-With-Long-Words thanks God for being imminent and transcendent. People begin to glaze over and count the bricks in the wall above the pulpit in order to stave off sleep and potentially embarrassing snoring incidents.

Sister Keep-it-Simple prays later in the meeting and reminds God that He's really magnificent and powerful, but thankfully He loves the small and insignificant. Brother Brick-Counter falls asleep during this eulogy, and the rest of the congregation ponder the sister's blessed thought (but are no closer to engaging with these two aspects of the character of God).

Next week Brother Word-Picture rises and reads from Isaiah 40: 11–12:

> He tends his flock like a shepherd
> He gathers the lambs in his arms
> And carries them close to his heart
> He gently leads those that have young
>
> Who has measured the waters in the hollow of his hand, or
> with the breadth of his hand, marked off the heavens?
> Who has held the dust of the earth in a bucket?
> Or weighed the mountains on the scales or the hills in a
> balance?

He goes on to remind his listeners that those same hands flung stars into space and were brutally maimed by the nails that held Him to the cross. He gently applies this to the current circumstances of people's lives, reminding them that the resources of the one who made the universe are those of the one who numbers the hairs of our heads and is our comfort in the darkest valley, whatever foolishness we may have indulged in and however ashamed we may be.

Gentle weeping from the back of the church rises from a knot of women comforting one who had never really known affirming, unconditional love from her family, and has felt revelation about the relentless mercy of God bloom in her heart in the previous minutes.

Talk of buckets, dust, shepherds, and beating hearts expresses the sublime in terms our mundane minds can grasp. A strong protecting shepherd/creator helps us "see" God in a way that terms such as "imminent" and "transcendent" never will.

CROSSING THE BRIDGE

Imagine Jesus had turned to the teacher of the law who quizzed Him as to who his neighbor was and simply said, "This'll shock you, but they include those Samaritans that you don't like." An interminable row then breaks out about the religious beliefs of Israel's neighbor, and the crowd, Jesus, and the aggressive religious leader all end up frustrated.

Instead, He tells the story of a Samaritan who rescues a dying man, even as people who should have come to his aid leave him to suffer. Jesus told stories and asked questions and, in doing so, started a process of thought that would change the pattern of people's thinking. It changed the way they thought because they reflected on information and real life situations and arrived at a conclusion, rather than having the conclusion simply declared to them.

I once sat with a musician as he prepared to sing to a group of musicians, poets, and writers. I encouraged him to sing a song called "It's hard to say goodnight," assured him he would get a response, and told him to be ready to counsel people.

He sang his song, which was the story of a couple very much in love. They should say goodnight and let the man go home. But the weather is bad and the room is cozy and they are awash in a sensual haze. The last verse encourages the listener to consider that whatever the pressures, and the pleasurable reality of temptation, it needs to be resisted, because a mistake made in a moment could haunt them for a lifetime.

He sang it, and sometime later, after talking at length to three people, he confirmed that I had been right. What were the strengths of the song? It opened up a discussion in a way that a blunt call to sexual abstinence may not have done. It said to the listener that the writer understood some of the realities of love and desire. It took them to the keep-it-for-marriage conclusion by a different route than a here-are-the-rules, just-keep-them approach, which demands obedience but doesn't promote understanding.

The Apostle Paul helped people cross the bridge of understanding one day on Mars Hill. He started with what they knew before introducing them to new concepts and ideas. He talked of their statue to an unknown god and reminded them of a poem about Zeus. He found a window of truth in their beliefs and began to connect it with the way, the truth, and the life.[2]

Every other major religion in the world is a corruption of the revelation of God, a distortion of the Creator's intent. They all usually have fragments of truth or insight among the error. Paul grasped some of those fragments and established a conversation, not a confrontation. Confrontation inevitably comes because the message of sin's corruption, Christ's death and the call to a life of worship is confrontational. Some scoffed at Paul's story of the resurrection, but others asked to hear more. Our initial conversations with people don't need to start with a provocation. Confrontation will eventually come because the message of sin's corruption, Christ's death, and the call to a life of worship is confrontational.

A Buddhist girl attended our church for some months. She had been involved with another local church, but was informed early in the relationship that Buddhism was demonic and she needed to renounce it now. Twenty-two years of her life were dismissed in a sentence, and the spiritual integrity of her entire network of friends and relatives was called into question. The response to that type of one-sentence judgment is always going to be hurt and anger.

I believe that Buddhism is a deception and that at a fundamental theological level, our friends in the church down the road were right. But we took a different approach. We talked to her about the eight-fold path of Buddhism and noted that some of their values were similar to those we held. We did not dismiss her experience out of hand. We emphasized, however, that we believed that there was a much bigger story about life than Buddhism was telling and that Christ had made unique claims about needing to follow Him if we wanted to discover God. She was treated with dignity, points of agreement and disagreement were noted, and nobody compromised their core beliefs. She felt welcome, valued, and respected and continued to explore the Christian faith for several months before returning to Japan.

A CULTURE CARRIER

Storytelling, using word pictures and discussing common experiences, is one way we both learn of truth and give it away to others. In the culture we live in, story remains at the core of shared cultural experiences. People talk about the reality TV shows they've watched, the sports matches they've been to, and the films they have seen.

Here is a challenge. Contemporary cinema explores all kinds of issues. *Saving Private Ryan* reflects on the emotional scars of war, *Pay it Forward* examines selfless behavior and personal sacrifice, *Star Wars* looks to Eastern philosophies of yin and yang as it explores the tension between darkness and light and good and bad. Many helpful books can help you explore the worldviews of today's films.[3]

But do some exploration yourself. Rent a movie that is culturally pervasive. I recommend *Aladdin*, the Walt Disney blockbuster from the early '90s.

As you watch this movie, ask yourself some questions.

- How is the heroine Jasmine drawn? Is it realistic?
- At that time, how common was the punishment Aladdin was due to suffer? How do you feel when extreme Christianity is portrayed as the norm?
- Aladdin rejects some girls in the story. Is it on the basis of their character? What message does the young viewer

receive from this part of the film?

I'll not tell you my conclusions, for that would defeat the object of the exercise. But if we take the time to reflect on the stories that are all around us, we begin to see their role in reinforcing values or ideas already held (how many films now portray premarital sex as normative?), introducing new ones, or, as was often the case with Jesus, subverting popular beliefs (the Samaritan is your neighbor).

When we don't tell stories, we end up with a sterile, joyless, rules, laws, and statements faith that neither nurtures the soul nor speaks to unbelievers.

Followers of Jesus will tell stories to make points, aid understanding, and build bridges of communication—and just for the sheer joy of telling and listening.

1. John 8:5
2. Acts 17:16-33
3. Brian Godawa, *Hollywood Worldviews* (IVP, 2002); Gareth Higgins, *How Movies Helped Save My Soul* (Relevant Books, 2003).

7

SWIMMING LESSONS WITH ST. PETER

As disciples go, Peter was a bit of a nightmare. He starts out of a boat to walk across the water to Jesus, only to feel the cold waters begin to envelop him. He sees Jesus on a mountain with Moses and Elijah, and his first thought is to build a monument. He swears he'll never betray Jesus and then denies knowing Him three times within the next twenty-four hours. He falls into a trance on a roof and argues with God about unclean animals and taking the message of Jesus to the other nations of the world.

Peter was, however, the rock on which the Church was built. He was eager to live the life to which Jesus was calling him, but as we've noted, made some mistakes along the way. His willingness to take a risk and sometimes fail meant he was more likely to succeed.

There is a pattern in Jesus relationship with His disciples that runs something like this:

- Watch, listen, enquire.
- Try it yourself.
- Succeed and sometimes fail.

- Receive advice.
- Try again.

Let's explore what this means and discover a second learning path: learning by doing.

WITHNESS

At the heart of Jesus' work life and relationship with the disciples lies a simple fact. He spent a lot of time with the disciples. They weren't always in the synagogue, feeding huge crowds, or healing people.

Jesus' "withness" with His disciples meant that informal conversation could flow, questions could be asked, and problems explored. Some of the time the disciples were asking, "What did you mean when you told that story earlier on?" But at other times the disciples weren't saying, "What?"; they were asking "How?"

Jesus never had it in mind to create a small band of followers who cheered Him on and kept the crowds under control. From day one He was training them to emulate what He had done and was doing. Indeed, He even suggests that His followers would do greater things, because He was going to return to His father.[1]

Two incidents in the book of Luke point us to a pattern that is key to understanding how we grow in our faith.

Jesus calls the twelve together and confers on them His authority to drive out all demons and cure diseases.[2] They are to travel with the minimum of baggage and no extra clothing, food, or money. They aren't to wander from house to house seeking support, but they are to preach about the kingdom and heal the sick. They had watched the Master at work. Now it is time for them to learn by doing.

A little while later, He gathers seventy-two of His other followers and sends them out to prepare the way for Him. Once again, they have explicit instruction about their conduct, clothing, and priorities. They are to declare peace, eat with people, pray for their healing, and declare that the kingdom of God is near.[3]

They return rejoicing, because even the demons submitted to them in the name of Jesus. He warns them to root their joy in the promises of God, not earthly power, but the lesson for us is clear. People can observe faith in action, but the time comes when they need to go out and do the deeds they've seen Him do.

They grew in confidence, but there were times when they encountered obstacles and difficulties and their faith wavered. They asked Jesus' advice, and He talked to them of faith and prayer and fasting.[4]

A CHALLENGE THAT CHANGES
Sometimes we are consumed by a carefulness that stops us from sending out our twelves and seventy-twos. We are waiting for them to be mature and seeking to create situations with little chance of failure.

We worry about people's age and insight, but the reality is this: The key biblical characters demonstrated their heart for God while children and young adults. They were at the very heart of the history of salvation, and they often learned by experience and faith.

Samuel responded to the voice of God, but only after mistaking it for the voice of Eli. He was then given prophetic insight that revealed the spiritual darkness at the heart of the nation.

Joseph had insight into the life of his clan, but was banished by his brothers and falsely accused by the wife of his master. He eventually became the governor of a nation, but only after years in jail.

Daniel's three young adult friends, Shadrach, Meshach, and Abednego, were far from the roots that nourished their faith, but they persisted, telling the king they would not renounce their faith, even if God did not come to their rescue when he had them executed via the fiery furnace.

David defied the might of an opposing army as a young adult. He refused to fear the Philistine giant and defended his nation.

Josiah was nurtured in the faith of his fathers and received special training from the age of eight. At sixteen he rid the land of idol worship and the child sacrifice and sexual promiscuity associated with the pagan religion that worshiped Baal and Ashteroth.

Jesus went to the temple at the age of twelve and engaged the high priests in debate, causing several to marvel at His knowledge and insight.

The thing to note in respect to all these lives is that they had been immersed in the faith of their people and had observed the everyday expressions of faith. There came a time, however, when they simply had to take that faith and let it inform their actions. They were learning by doing.

IMMERSION LEARNING

I once worked with a charity that established projects which would earn money that could be given away to help the poor. For the first few years, people set up temporary restaurants in the weeks before Christmas. People were encouraged to "eat less, pay more." In later years we established twenty-eight-day radio stations. We wanted to earn money so we could provide people in other nations with food and clothes and help them toward a sustainable future.

But actually we were on a massive "learning by doing" exercise. We were learning about food preparation, media skills, publicity, and team building. We were discovering a biblical view of justice together as we considered the reasons why we were undertaking the projects. We were learning about being servant-hearted. We were being sensitized to injustice and the pain of others.

We were preparing a generation of young Christians to express God's love in word and in deed. We were undertaking the good works God had prepared in advance for us to do.[5]

But in many cases, we didn't start as experts. We had workbooks and handbooks to get us started. We sponsored training days to help people get started, but we learned by doing.

My father's legacy is full of learning by doing and is partly found in the lives of six young men. They discovered Christ in a meaningful way as they listened to Billy Graham. Their new pastor, a fresh-faced twentysomething at the time, got them together once a week and taught them the things he had learned at college. They stood and stuttered through their first public talks, they persevered during half nights of prayer and they listened carefully to what this man, only seven or eight years their senior, told them.

After two years, my dad had to move on, but his friendship with these young men endured for more than forty years, as he continued to train them, talk to them, and often just sit around relaxing with them.

They learned by doing. Two of them went on to lead the church. Another is a minister in a Pentecostal church. One leads a vocational Christian group, and the other has been a prominent figure in the Christian community in Japan for nearly two decades. These influences come from a hundred-strong church in a deprived area of London. They observed, and then they began to experiment and learn.

THE POWER OF CURIOSITY

If you motivate the heart, then the desire to learn skills often follows. Children, excited by the challenge of computer games, scorn the manual and learn by trial and error and research and hints from friends. As an adult, I learned to use the computer by simply setting out to do a task, such as writing a letter, and then finding out what I needed to do.

As you continue on your journey of faith, let the passion of your heart be the light that illuminates the learning paths you pursue. For some a careful overview of the four Gospels, systematically undertaken, is the way to discover their Savior, but for me it's often been via curiosity.

I asked our small group one night what we knew about Jesus and food. The answers tumbled out of them. He multiplied it; He cooked it for His disciples; He made extra wine; He ate with people whom others disapproved of; He celebrated the symbolic Passover meal; He told stories about food and banquets and parties.

The ordinary and the mundane were all part of the profound moments in Jesus' life. I was curious now and spent the next few weeks looking for books on Jesus and community. I discovered that Jesus' attitude toward food was part of His conflict with the religious people of His day. Nearly two-thirds of the extra rules they had added to the Scripture concerned food purity. Purity in their eyes was a key to holiness. Holiness was the key to deliverance by a conquering Messiah.

Jesus wasn't just eating food; He was defining the core of faith as being rooted in compassion in action. He was doubting the ability of man-made rules to keep us holy. He was accepting those whom others rejected.

My curiosity was a better teacher for me. I was engaged with the learning process. I wanted to know why Jesus made counter-cultural statements by sitting down to eat with civil servants and fishermen.

Are you waiting for spiritual insight to simply arrive in your mind? Are you waiting for that moment when you feel adequate to the task of serving God or taking responsibility within your church or Christian community?

Stop. And then start.

Stop waiting to be perfect or enlightened or mature. Start "doing the stuff," as the preacher John Wimber used to say. You'll learn by doing the small and commonplace. Ask a friend over for a relaxed night and help them feel at home in your community. Say a thirty-second prayer for someone facing a challenge in the coming days. Offer to sell sweets at the youth club night or be an extra helper in the Sunday school.

I've been told so many times (so it must be true!) that many leading figures in church were children's ministry volunteers in their young adult years. They became immersed in the foundations of their faith because they had to be ready to pass it on to the children in their care. They learned by doing.

Spirituality isn't usually expressed in the heroic, although it can be. Its whisper is heard in the word of encouragement, the warm greeting, the tone of forgiveness.

Doing takes us from being spectators to whole person involvement. It tests our faith and expands our knowledge.

Do the stuff. Follow Jesus.

1. John 14:12
2. Luke 9:1-6
3. Luke 10:5-9
4. Mark 9:14-29; Matthew 17:19-21
5. Ephesians 2:10

8

AN ANCIENT AND FUTURE FAITH

I'd like to tell you four stories. They're the stories of how my mind has heard whispers and shouts from the ancients, echoing across the centuries to speak to me as I seek to follow Jesus.

THE RAGGED CHURCH

Standing in the road outside an inner city church, a five-year-old wondered aloud: "Why are we moving these chairs?"

"We're having special meetings," came the reply. Up the stairs he went, seeking more explanation from his mother. "We want people to give their lives to Jesus," she told him.

"Why?" he asked. She explained, and minutes later he prayed a prayer of commitment.

The church was the Princess Louise Institute. It was named after a daughter of the British Queen Victoria. It had been established by Lord Shaftesbury, a campaigning Christian who established "Ragged" schools across London to help poor working class children receive an education. Several of the schools were established alongside new churches.

The boy was me, and my experience point us to our third learning path: the ancient stories of faith.

Shaftesbury was a pivotal figure in British politics. He campaigned against the child labor endemic in British cities and helped turn the medieval conditions in prisons into something more humane.[1] He was a significant figure in the arrival of safe sewerage and waste disposal arrangements and the consequent arrival of cleaner water in London.

He pioneered education for the ordinary child and established churches in urban areas that meet to this day. The organization that bears his name, the Shaftesbury Society, is a leading provider of affordable housing and specialist housing for the disabled. The legacy he left still speaks today.

As I entered my twenties, I began to search for Christian writers who would help me understand how my faith might relate to the everyday world of politics, business, and social justice. I discovered Jim Wallis (*The Cost of Conversion*) and Ronald Sider (*Rich Christians in Age of Hunger*), but hit the motherlode when I looked back into my own personal history and sought out biographies of Lord Shaftesbury and an earlier campaigner, William Wilberforce.

Wilberforce campaigned against slavery for forty years and is credited as the founder of the modern political campaign. He raised petitions, circulated leaflets, held local meetings, and persevered for four decades. He was an early campaigner against cruelty to animals, believing that the same mentality found in slave owners was found in those who beat or neglected animals, and that all aspects of God's creation needed protection from those who might abuse it.

The deeper I dug, the more I realized that those who believed God had made humanity in His own image, given mankind dignity and opportunities to live wise and worshipful lives, were the ones who had shaped in a positive way what we called civilization.

As a late twentieth century Christian, I was tempted to regard Christianity as marginal. I was not aware of its formative role in education, medical care for all, the abolition of slavery, the creation of humane justice, and simple things like adequate sanitation and clean water.

There were rich precedents for the impulse to justice I felt. Jesus had been announced to a marginal group, the shepherds. He had befriended another marginal group, the tax collectors. He had announced that He had come to speak for the poor.

Jesus' disciples had maintained that impulse across the millennia with a strong association between revival and renewal, prayer, and social compassion. Wilberforce had been profoundly influenced by Methodist pioneer Wesley. Shaftesbury was influenced by D.L. Moody, who had come from the streets of Chicago to reach out to ordinary men and women around the world.

I needed to hear of the ancients to make sense of my present. And what was true then is true now. The Viva Network, a forum for Christians working with children in need around the world, would have a bigger budget than the United Nations UNICEF project on behalf of children, were all the members to add all their annual budgets together.

The Christian Church is the most influential force for good in the world today, whatever its health in some parts of the world. Looking back will help us as we look forward and seek to serve our communities.

THE CULTURALLY PRESENT CHURCH

I have a friend, now in her seventies, who went to a Youth for Christ rally because she heard that the evangelists were good-looking Americans who dressed well. She came to faith that night in a small town hall. Hundreds of people have subsequently come to know Christ through her life and witness.

Years later though, she would fret as her sons went out to church events in jeans, baseball jackets, and Hawaiian shirts. She had connected culturally in her generation, but was a little wary of how a new generation were dressing for church. There is a temptation to insist on our version of witness as the definitive story, but each new generation will take the core stories of faith and present them in new places and in new forms.

Further back in history, an English missionary in China chafed at the segregation that seemed to exist between those who came with a message and those who were supposed to hear it. The missionaries lived with their own nationality, ate their traditional home food, and dressed as Westerners.

Hudson Taylor eventually revolted. He adopted Chinese clothes, ate with the Chinese, and went to live with them. Despite stiff opposition from other missionaries, he persevered and, with the support of his wife Maria, went on to help create the climate that has led to more than 50 million Chinese being Christians today.

I read about him in *Hudson Taylor and Maria* and felt an immediate connection.[2] I was twenty-five at the time and deeply involved in Christian music. I was beginning to get a little wary of the "we do it because it works" argument. I wanted to discover patterns in Church history and Scripture that would help me help others as they sought to use their creativity to the glory of God.

Hudson Taylor was a clue. He was a giant of the Church. Arguing that Christian music sought to cross the bridge into the lives of another people group, in the way that he did, got more of a response than "seventy got saved." The problem with the "seventy got saved" argument was that it begged many questions about what they had responded to and whether you could find them a few weeks later. Talking about music as a communication tool, not a salvation-inducing commodity, felt more satisfying.

Like all these things, the seed of thought grew. If Hudson Taylor sought to speak the cultural and verbal tongue of those he reached, was he reflecting an overall biblical truth?

You can't help but think so. We have four Gospels. Mark is the slightly breathless first account. Luke the historian gives us more depth. Matthew emphasizes Jesus' roots in Jewish culture, and John reflects on the teaching that would have a resonance in the lands to which the disciples traveled on their journey.

The disciples were no strangers to the mother tongue idea. Overcome by the Holy Spirit, they had spoken in the languages of many nations on the Day of Pentecost. The strange thing about this story relates to the fact that they were speaking to Jews up in Jerusalem for a festival. Why not speak in Aramaic?

Many of the pilgrims visiting Jerusalem would be second or third generation inhabitants of their new homes throughout the inhabited world. The disciples spoke to them in the language of their everyday conversation, not the words of their grandparents.

Paul, facing the philosophically diverse crowds on Mars Hill, spoke of their poets and gods, establishing a ground for discussion, before talking of Christ.

Understanding our roots takes us back to first principles, possibly obscured by the culture of our churches of society. The apostles or Hudson Taylor did not change the message, but they communicated it in ways that felt familiar and welcoming to people.

THE POWER OF A PRAYING PEOPLE

Some of my spiritual roots are in Methodism. When you dig deeper into Methodism, you find that much contemporary church practice is a representation of classic ideas from Wesley. Small groups or cells were an important part of the discipleship and maturing process for his early followers. His brother was a prolific hymnwriter, at a time when the Church had only just begun to move away from the metrical Psalms.

Bob Dylan produced a unique sound. But he was influenced by Woody Guthrie and Elvis Presley. Wesley produced a unique church, but he too was influenced by his own encounters with others. He had been moved by the resilience and faith of the Moravian Christians he encountered on a stormy voyage from the U.S. to England. Their calm servant-like attitude in the severest of storms provoked Wesley's spiritual curiosity and led him to the meeting in the Fetter Lane Moravian meeting house where his faith moved from his head to his heart and he found himself "strangely warmed."

I had known this for a long time, but had never really researched the influence of Zinzendorf and the Moravians on the fledgling faith of the Wesleys. About three years ago, I became aware of a group of young people who were encouraging churches to set aside seven days to pray twenty-four hours per day. I met Pete Greig, a founding member of the 24-7 prayer movement, and as we talked, I resolved to find out more about the Moravians who were inspiring a movement that has now sparked more than 1,500 prayer rooms in fifty nations. The journey of discovery, like several before it has challenged the way I perceive my faith and affirmed things I had been reflecting on for years.

Wesley traveled to Germany to visit the fount of this spiritual renewal and discovered the Hernnhut, a community of believers living under the protection of Count Nicolas Zinzendorf. The Count had organized his church into "bands" according to age and sex. These small groups met daily to encourage each other. The whole community would also meet often simply to sing, drawing on the prolific lyrical output of the Count.

In 1727, after reconciliation in the sometimes-divided community following a special communion service, Zinzendorf encouraged the single people to "pray without ceasing." They took one-hour slots, and with forty-eight people involved, they took part every two days. The spiritual passion that arose had to find an outlet, and in 1732 the Moravians began to send out evangelists, first to the Caribbean and Greenland, and soon all over the world.

The continuous prayer was to continue for more than one hundred years and spark the flame that was to become the modern missionary movement.

Small groups, hymn singing, and mission to the unreached were all to be hallmarks of Methodism. Zinzendorf's spiritual children were to have greater influence than he did, but his legacy lived on through their work.

As is often the case, you go back to your roots only to then add new dimensions to the information you find there. In *Red Moon Rising*, Pete and I outline the wide variety of prayer that takes place in these highly decorated prayer rooms some have put together.[3] The new takes you by surprise, as you're encouraged to pray holding massive nails like those that might have pierced Jesus. Your eyes widen as you approach a wall covered in silver foil and dotted with prayer requests from non-Christians with whom the church is in contact. Your sixty minutes flies by as you move from prayer activity to prayer activity. Ever so often, you step back through the centuries to an ancient prayer idea.

You're encouraged to read Psalm 103 slowly and to then select a verse to read and reflect on. You alight on the words of hope that flow from the idea that God is slow to anger and abounding in mercy. You're partaking in a tradition known as Lectio Divinia. Amid the color and creativity of this twenty-first century prayer room, you connect again with the Church fathers who passed on the wisdom that is transforming your life even as you pray. When you entered the room, you may have been through the Ignatian practice of Examen. This three-part process involves adoration, confession, and thanksgiving and finds you involved in a symbolic hand washing, a time of praise, and a time of simple thanksgiving. The past once again touched your present and influenced your future.

Wesley led me to Zinzendorf, who lead me even further into the annals of church history to discover truth for today.

WALK ON THE WILD SIDE

The family tree was a thing of wonder. It went back to the 1770s and included a family member who had come to faith at a meeting at which Wesley was to have spoken. My ancient great, great … grandfather, there to hear Wesley, was still impressed by the former vagrant who took the ill evangelist's place and began a journey of faith that still touches a Northern Ireland community today. He planted a Methodist church as his faith grew, and that congregation has worshiped near Belfast for more than 230 years. His son was to grow wary of the changes that swept Methodism following the death of the founder and yearned for a return to the involvement of all in the life of the Church, rather than the dominance of the professional clergy that had become the norm. He joined with thirty-three other churches in a new grouping.

They were influenced by an American called Lorenzo Dow. Lorenzo took the encouraging story of my faith roots in a new and provocative direction. He visited Ireland often and so impressed my family members that they named a son after him. Lorenzo Dow Cunningham helped establish a Bible college and sparked my curiosity nearly two hundred years later. Who was this man who had so impacted my family?

Lorenzo Dow was one of the most famous men of his generation, and more than 20,000 God-fearing parents around the world named their children after him. Known to many as "Crazy" Dow, he was a striking figure whose long hair and all black clothing were but the first two clues that here was someone different. Banished to an out-of-the-way Canadian church by conservative Methodists, he saw the congregation increase by 500 percent before returning to the U.S. and helping plant the first Protestant churches in five American states.

He was deeply moved by the Cane Ridge camp meeting revival of 1801, which was marked by fiery preaching, prayer, prostration, and spiritual fervor. He urged his friends around the globe to consider the possibility of holding outdoor camp meetings and helped hasten the arrival of the pioneering Primitive Methodists as a result.

The Primitives gathered on a Shropshire hillside and preached and prayed for several days. Summoned to account for their actions by the Methodist authorities of the time, they protested that they were simply "primitive" Methodists seeking to emulate Wesley. The phrase stuck, and a denomination that would attract a crowd of 100,000 to a nineteenth century prayer meeting was born. They believed in the active work of the Holy Spirit in supernatural gifts and were particularly influenced by a Quaker Methodist called Crawfoot.

Hugh Bourne, a founder of the Primitives, Lorenzo Dow, and Crawfoot are going to be a fertile field of discovery for me for some time to come as I discover the prayer strategies, Christian nurture ideas and love for Christ that fueled these risk-taking men. I never want to be wild for the sake of it, simply as a pose or posture, but there is something deeply appealing about the simple determination of Lorenzo Dow. My past speaks again to my future.

NEVER FORGET

The Psalmist warming to his theme in Psalm 78:1-6 tells us what he is going to do:

I will open my mouth in parables,
I will utter hidden things, things from of old
what we have heard and known,
what our fathers have told us.
We will not hide them from their children;
we will tell the next generation
the praiseworthy deeds of the LORD ,
his power, and the wonders he has done.
He decreed statutes for Jacob
and established the law in Israel,
which he commanded our forefathers
to teach their children,
so the next generation would know them,
even the children yet to be born,

and they in turn would tell their children.

The stories of the past are a rich resource for us. They will not provide exact blueprints, but they will embody principles or lead us to perspectives that are new to us.

I have discovered the roots of my faith through my family history, in much the same way as the psalmist urges above. Not all will be able to do that, but you will find the lives of those who inspire your church, and the heroes of the faith that you are yet to discover, are a rich source of precedent and inspiration as to how you might follow Jesus.

1. Shaftesbury, *John Pollock* (Kingsway Publications, 2001).
2. John Pollock, *Hudson Taylor* and *Maria*
3. Pete Greig & Dave Roberts, *Red Moon Rising* (Relevant Books, 2003).

9

GIVE ME THAT OLD TIME RELIGION

Memories are like the mile markers at the side of the road of life. They tell you how you're progressing and how much closer to home you're getting. Learning to remember is our fourth learning path.

Memories are sensual too. They relate to every one of the five senses. As a boy I often attended soccer matches with crowds of up to 30,000. We stood on concrete terraces and savored the smell of the ground, a curious mixture of roasted chestnuts, food odors, cigarette and cigar smoke, and the aroma of several thousand men.

We shivered in the cold, our already strained nerves set on edge by the game and further tightened by the sheer physicality of our environment. When the team needed encouragement, twenty voices would start to sing, and on some occasions, all 30,000 would join in the acapella thunder that would roll around the ground.

For some, this fortnightly ritual became their church. The money spent on merchandising was their tithe, the songs and chant their liturgies, and memorable matches their special festivals.

They formed friendships there, married at the grounds, and were consumed by their passion for the game and the traditions they observed at the weekly gatherings—some traveled around the country for the away matches. Their lives had a steady beat. They played familiar opponents, and the season had a predictable rhythm: friendlies, then league matches and entry into the various cup competitions.

Tradition intrudes into our lives quite often. My father started a tradition of gathering the young men from the church he had lead on the evening of Christmas day. They had spent time with their families but withdrew before the heavy drinking or revelry set in. A decade after Dad had left the church, they still came pouring through the door ready to eat a Christmas meal and then play Monopoly. It was a delicious thrill for a ten-year-old to stay up after his normal bedtime talking and competing with these adults and joining in their ready laughter and relaxed friendship. It became both a tradition and a memory.

Tradition can also be a part of your personal landscape, hardly noticed or thought about until one of those divine moments when it suddenly comes to life. I stood one day in the 6,000-strong crowd at a Christian music festival. The communion service was unfolding before us, and we were invited to come and receive the bread and the wine. This familiar and often unremarkable tradition suddenly became alive for me as I stood in line. Gazing around the crowd in one of those unguarded moment where you are reflecting and simply perceiving what is all around, I started to choke up, tears rising to my eyes and a sob to my throat.

The body that had been broken for me had produced this body of people all around me—the Body of Christ. The sense I often had of being a member of a tiny minority, despised by the wider culture and desperately seeking to make sense of ancient truth and modern life, was replaced by this sense of wonder. I stood in the midst of this multitude of believers, united both in the remembrance of Christ's life and death, but also in their desire to communicate faith in a creative way to the wider culture. I felt I belonged.

Tradition is often a mixture of familiar ritual and memorable landmarks. They become intermingled, the one reminding us of the other. The Israelites celebrated the Passover, giving thanks to God, but it was a constant evocation of the Exodus and their delivery from the bonds of Egyptian oppression.

The soccer team I support, Charlton Athletic, is an everyday case in point, and its story reminds us of three key things about our traditions.

IT TELLS A STORY THAT SHAPES OUR VALUES

In 1984 the team was virtually bankrupt. The members were forced to leave their grounds and share facilities with others whose grounds were often many miles from the place where the majority of the supporters lived. Several key figures among the supporters decided to mount a campaign for a return to The Valley, their south London ground.

A fan at a leading international advertising agency prepared the campaign materials and the fans formed a political party which stood in the wards and boroughs where politicians were obstructing the team's return. The Valley Party split the Labour vote and changed the face of local politics. Their point made, they disbanded, but the return to the ground was now ensured.

The club called for volunteers to help restore the ground, and on one windswept Sunday, more than 1,000 fans arrived at the ground amid great emotion. In 1992 the club played there again. By 2007, The Valley will be one of the biggest capacity grounds in the U.K.

The club's whole identity has been shaped by those years. It's renowned as the club who came back from near death to reach its current top six status. But the lessons of the '80s linger. Because a community had its club taken away, the club now values the community in a deliberate and intentional way with multitudes of sporting and educational schemes sponsored by the team. Because the club was rescued by its fans, who were drawn from every sector of local society, the club values all its fans, campaigning vigorously against racism in the ground and outside it.

Because the club nearly died because of debt, the club is managed very prudently and is now one of the few top clubs in Europe not collapsing under a mountain of debt.

You can distill the story into a paragraph. We lost our ground. We refused to bow down to this. We campaigned in a strategic way. We got our ground back. We have a special relationship with our fans. We won't get into that kind of debt again.

Each year the mythology is reinforced with a "Back to The Valley" dinner, and on the tenth anniversary, our more than 1,000 fans walked the route of one of the key protest marches.

The traditions tell a story; they create a community of shared memory and a narrative that is remembered, referred to in discussion of the club's future, and passed on to future generations. One father told me of taking his son to see the derelict ground and the son's surprise when he broke down and cried as he saw the chaos that had overtaken this place of memory and celebration. Five years later, they returned for the first match back at the former stadium, and once again this grown man wept. His son couldn't understand why, but for the father, it was a renewal of hope. Seven years later, the team won promotion in one of the most thrilling matches of the last twenty years, and the father turned to his weeping son and said, "Now do you understand?"

LOSING OUR COLLECTIVE MEMORY

Those who follow Jesus might be in danger of losing our traditions and all the memories and associations that go with them as we seek the new and innovative. Jesus, however, affirmed tradition and all it evoked in the midst of His own personal spiritual innovation and His declared wariness of that which was mere observance or legalism.

One key biblical tradition serves to illustrate the power of both symbol and memory. As Joshua lead his people to freedom across the Jordan, God instructed him to have a man from each tribe take a stone from the riverbed and place them together in a memorial. Joshua then instructed the people that when their children in later years enquire as to the meaning of the stones, they were to tell the story of God cutting off the flow of the Jordan as the Ark of the Covenant passed over. The stones were to be a memorial of God's deliverance forever.[1]

The stones evoked a story. They created a narrative that captured the idea of God's passion and put in place a common memory that shaped the lives of future generations.

The Passover meal was the same, mixing as it did eating and ritual prayer. The meal can take as long as six hours, and involves the tactile symbolism of bitter herbs and unleavened bread. The participants remember the pain of captivity and the joy of release and deeply internalize the idea of God who comes to set the captives free.

The Passover was no isolated meal or tradition. In time, several festivals entered the rhythm of religion in the life of the Israelite.

> Passover–remembrance of deliverance.
> Trumpet Blowing–a day of rest.
> Feast of Weeks–celebration of the first fruits and gathering of the people.
> Feast of Booths–celebration of harvest.
> The Sabbath–a weekly day of rest.
> Day of Atonement–a special time of repentance.
> Purim–a day of remembrance of historical deliverance–it involved feasting and gladness.

The other festivals in the Near East often involved sorrow, followed by joy, but the Hebrews did not have that sharp distinction and would have sometimes mourn and repent in the midst of their most joyous celebrations. The feasts and festivals had several functions:

REMEMBERING GOD'S FAVOR

The Passover meal was to be eaten in a state of readiness for departure. The Deliverer was coming. Your staff should be at hand, your sandals on your feet, and your cloak tucked into your belt.[2]

SAVORING GOD'S FAVOR

Personal enjoyment was a key aspect of these festivals. The people are invited to eat choice fruit and gather foliage for use in their festival of rejoicing.[3]

BEING RECONCILED

The traditions often involved the sacrifice of something of value as a symbol of repentance. This in turn led to reconciliation with God.[4]

JESUS AND REMEMBRANCE

Jesus and His followers remained immersed in the traditions of their people and give us an example to follow.

With His family, Jesus went annually to Jerusalem to celebrate the Passover. He celebrated the Passover with His disciples and transformed it into a meal that would evoke the memory of a second deliverance, not merely from the power of the Egyptians but from the power of sin and death and hell. It's clear from the Gospels that Jesus traveled to Jerusalem to participate in the feasts and that the people anticipated He would be there.[5]

Jesus and the disciples also strongly identified with the prayer rituals of the Hebrews. He provokes the teacher of the law to speak to Him the first and last words of the Schema, a daily prayer of the devout Jew, based on passages from the Old Testament. Jesus also declared this same prayer formula when pressed by another teacher of the law, telling him that to love God with all your heart, soul, mind and strength and to love your neighbor as yourself was the greatest commandment.[6]

We later find the disciples worshiping daily at the temple and participating in the three-times-per day prayers that took place there. As Peter and John arrived at the temple for three o'clock prayers, a man who asked for money received a healing instead, and a new chapter opened up for the disciples, as they had both the opportunity to preach and found themselves in conflict with the local religious authorities.[7]

The role of tradition, symbol, and memory in salvation history has much to say to us, whether we seek to follow Jesus, or are indeed just seekers.

GIVING US A STORY

While many Christians can recount the basic story of the cross, their sense of how the rest of the biblical narrative fits can be sketchy. This is amplified by a culture of innovation that seeks only the "now" word of God and distances itself from tradition, remembrance, the Christian seasons, and liturgy.

Communion services, Easter celebrations, the Christmas carol service, Sunday school anniversaries, and annual church camps are all part of a potential tradition of festivals, rituals, and symbols that give us a sense of where we stand in the history of salvation. They can provide powerful visual symbols, as can services of dedication and baptism. The possibility of rites-of-passage celebrations for the soon-to-be teenager are increasingly being explored by many Christians, as are weekly family meals that include worship, prayer, Bible reading, and reflection.

CONNECTING WITH THE PRESENT; CONNECTING WITH THE PAST

Social mobility and family breakdown have left many with a reduced sense of their heritage or the potential wisdom they might discover from their past. This rootless feeling could have been a scourge for the wandering Israelites, but their habitual return to the great themes of their faith and their use of visual symbolism, such as the stories at Gilgal, meant that the stories of faith passed from generation to generation. This helped shape decisions in the present.

NO LONGER ALONE

All of these traditions infer community, gathering, and belonging and undermine the idea of a privatized faith that isn't expressed through participation in a community of believers. The Church, with its predictable cycles of remembrance and reflection, becomes a safe place where people may have their ideas challenged but can find friendship, festivity, and the stories that will make sense of all the human condition.

Being a follower of Jesus will introduce you to living traditions that will touch every part of your life. What cycles of remembrance do you want to help innovate in your church?

1. Joshua 4
2. Exodus 12
3. Leviticus 23
4. Numbers 28
5. Luke 2:41, 22:8; John 5:1, 7:2, 11:55-56
6. Mark 12:28-34; Luke 10:26-28.
7. Luke 24:53; Acts 3

10

HEROES OF THE FAITH

You and God. Intimate, loving friends. Walking and talking every day. That's how it was for Adam, so that's the way it should be now, shouldn't it? Well, maybe. The maybe could become a definite yes, but only if the both/and principle comes into play. We need our own conversations with God and the example of others.

Let's contrast for a moment differing perspectives about God, Jesus, and the Holy Spirit. We can regard God as a majestic ruler, distant and regal, approached with a timid deference. In recent times, this cold, austere God has been set aside in favor of a caring, compassionate God. We can imagine Him holding us in His arms like a gentle shepherd.[1] We believe that He was made visible to us in Jesus, who touched the maimed, the lame, the leper, and the prostitute, using everyday contact to model the love of the heavenly Father.

So far, so good. But perhaps there's a stumbling block waiting for us. Many of us desire explicit experiences to help validate our faith. This might be anything from a miracle healing to a "word from God," right through to visionary experiences or a sense of well being. None of these things are wrong, and Scripture suggests they were part of the everyday experience of the disciples of Jesus. They prayed for a man at the Gate Beautiful, Peter had a vision on the roof of a house, they were constantly thankful, and Paul received a missionary call to Macedonia in a dream.

The problem arises when these experiences become our focus. We can start to doubt our faith if it's not validated by regular semi-mystical moments. Perhaps more subtle, however, is the temptation to elevate personal emotional experience to the prime position in forming our character and spirituality. "If only I could meet with God in a fresh way, my life would change."

This is not reality. This is a dream state that desires spiritual shortcuts. The reality is you have to be marinated in goodness, not just coated in it.

It takes a church to marinate a Christian. Jesus gave us a pattern. He had one best friend, John. He had three close friends, James, John, and Peter. He had twelve disciples, and at least seventy other key followers. His example spread like a virus from one life to another. This is the fifth learning path: the example of others.

MAKING THINGS PLAUSIBLE

Imagine for a moment that you're Peter. What are you going to learn from the other disciples and those, including Paul, who would follow Jesus in the years of His life and the decades after His death? What in their lives will speak to yours? What kind of example will they be to you, and what kind of example will you be to them?

Opening up our hearts and minds to the possibility of learning from the example of others is an act of worship. It says to God and others that we do not regard ourselves as the sources of all knowledge that will guide our lives. It acknowledges the possibility of wisdom from others. It suggests a desire to connect with others that is the foundation of community. It suggests humility.

Following the example of others is a Christian instinct. It echoes the behavior of Jesus.

"I tell you the truth, the Son can do nothing by himself; he can do only what he sees his Father doing, because whatever the Fathers does the Son also does."[2]

Jesus in turn urges the disciples to follow His example and to deny themselves, take up their crosses, and follow Him.[3] This may involve humility and service. Jesus reminds the disciples after washing their feet that He has set an example they should follow.[4] Paul carries on this idea of looking to the past and present for clues to the future when he urges the Corinthians to be imitators of him, just as he is an imitator of Christ.[5]

So what can we learn from our friends? And how do we learn?

THE EMBODIMENT OF IDEAS
Much of what we learn from others is "caught" rather than taught. We observe a person's life, their vision, and their plans, and we orient our life in that direction.

After many years of involvement in a wild Pentecostal church, I wanted to find a church that honored our God-given minds, but still had a radical commitment to the work of the Holy Spirit today. Over the years I had met Martyn, a local church leader, several times and knew he sought to combine these values. He had loaned me books on how one might discover a Christian worldview that spoke to all aspects of our lives. I joined his church and now serve alongside him on the leadership team. I caught the virus of his ideas.

I felt the same way about the Christian leader John Wimber. His Vineyard movement welcomed the work of the Holy Spirit, but their conferences and publications suggested a careful thoughtfulness and a commitment to the whole person that I could follow. He was warm-hearted toward those who shaped some of his vision but perhaps worshiped in other traditions. He encouraged the arts and social compassion. He embodied several ideals or ideas I had been examining.

Our examples in the arena of ideas help make our faith plausible. They suggest that we are not alone in our insights and that these ideas can find expression in a community of faith.

Have you found an example in the arena of ideas? Is there someone whose insights you admire? Have you found someone who is modeling church life and personal faith to you? This book is about how Jesus embodied the idea of the love of God. If you are to be a long-term disciple of Jesus, you will need to find a person who embodies your Christian ideals and let their ideas help shape your mind and character.

THE PROVOCATION OF ACTION

I have a friend named Pete Greig. He's a wild and hard to tame kind of man. He can plan and strategize with the best of us, but he also likes to just see what happens.

He once traveled around Europe looking for the provocation of the Spirit and visiting friends. He had to pretend it was a holiday to make it legitimate in the eyes of some, but actually he was stepping out in faith, hoping for a word from God.

He eventually reached the Hernnhut, home of the Moravian church, and the site of a 100-year prayer meeting. The century-long prayer chain began with forty-eight young people and eventually provoked 3,000 to take the Christian story around the world.

Wandering around this rural German town, anonymous to the world and famous only to Christians as the home of a pioneering church, Pete came to believe that perhaps his church should try to pray twenty-four hours a day, seven days a week for one month. If The Hernnhuters could do 100 years, surely they could do a month.

Friends from visiting churches liked the idea, and before long, other prayer rooms had sprung up. There have now been over 1,500 prayer rooms in more than fifty countries.

Pete is an example to me and many others, not just because he's rediscovered some ancient ideas about prayer, but because he's taken risks.

Prayer teams now go to important places within youth and young adult culture, such as Ibiza and Aiya Nappa, the summer dance capitals of Europe. A constant prayer vigil is complemented by prayer on the streets, acts of practical kindness, and DJ spots in the local clubs.

Back home, some cities have begun to explore the idea of third millennium monasteries. Prayer goes on constantly, but it is the hub of a wheel that includes a wide variety of activities, including youth clubs and work with young people excluded from school.[6]

Pete has new ideas regularly. Some of them will fail. Others touch the world. One night sitting in the prayer room, he wrote a poem that became know as "The Vision."[7] It's now been read by more than 1 million people.

The prayer rooms put together by Pete and his friends are a multi-sensory adventure. You scribble prayer on walls, symbolically cleanse yourself by washing your hands, quietly eat bread and drink wine, and noisily cry out to God for the lost and broken. The secret of these rooms is that they're very low tech. It all packs away into a box. You can do it all yourself with fabric, pens, paper, blu-tack, maps, paintbrushes, and pins.

The idea of a prayer room where you pray alone for sixty minutes becomes viable to many people, when faced with twelve prayer ideas that will take five minutes each. Pete and his friends led by example. They provoked us to action by making the idea of an hour alone with God seem possible and creative.

CATCHING THEIR CHARACTER

You can't classify everything into neat little boxes and tidy lists. But I do believe that through our lives we can suggest patterns. Being friends with people gives us a chance to observe how they handle joy, sorrow, conflict, loss, and the everyday pressures of life, the workplace, or the family.

Sometimes they will help us know how to respond. At other times they will help us unlearn previous patterns of thought and give credibility to new ways.

I have a friend who suffered from rage. He had attended many schools and seen his parents estranged. People at his college were literally scared of him, but one student offered him friendship. He had my friend's respect because he was as athletic as him and didn't seem scared. He began to have another way of living modeled to him in a consistent way over many months. Perhaps for the first time, he spent a lot of time in the company of someone who did not model anger as a response to life's difficulties.

He committed his life to Jesus and asked for the kind of "heart" surgery that would get to the root of his wounded spirit and bring healing. A man was restored because another man simply modeled, perhaps without even realizing it, another way of living.

I once attended soccer matches for three seasons with a friend from our youth club. In three seasons he never got into trouble with the police. The season after I left to go to college he got arrested eight times. He had caught my character while I was there, but had not wanted to risk the wrath of his family by exploring the Christian faith.

People catch our character. At the very least it may restrain them. At best it provokes the deep curiosity that leads to wanting to know more about Jesus.

LEARNING THE TRICKS OF THE TRADE

How did Jesus learn to be a carpenter? He simply watched Joseph and then copied him. No doubt Joseph advised and illustrated, but Jesus would have observed much of the technique and simply copied it.

Sometimes we watch our pastor at work in the faith discovery class. As he responds to the hard questions of curious agnostics or seeks to give thoughtful responses to questions about earth's origins, I store away the comments for later recycling in other conversations.

My mentor as a magazine editor once praised my business plan for a new project, affirmed his commitment to it, and then asked several hard questions. He sent me away to find the answers so we could anticipate the questions of the board members even before they asked them.

I learned something that day about being thorough. I learned something that day about the value of affirmation. Affirmed and encouraged, I was ready to hear the difficult questions.

Sometimes what you learn is simply a sentence or a paragraph, but it helps you organize the way you think and work. Jesus gave the disciples a few sentences about prayer to help them discover a liturgy for their own prayers. While at college, I heard a simple teaching that has shaped my speaking ever since.

They told us to tell the listener what we planned to cover. Then tell them. Then remind them what we had just spoken of. They also told us to explain the Bible in its context, then draw out some principles, and then apply them to everyday life.

They are simple thoughts, but they shape your life.

You need times when you commune with God. But quiet moments and a Sunday service will not be enough on their own to stoke the spiritual engines. You catch the fire from others.

Following Jesus means valuing friendship, community, and the wisdom of others.

1. Isaiah 40:11-12
2. John 5:19
3. Mark 8:34
4. John 13:15
5. 1 Corinthians 11:1
6. Find out more at *www.24-7prayer.com*.
7. Read more about "The Vision" in *Red Moon Rising* by Pete Greig and Dave Roberts (Relevant Books, 2003).

11

HABITS OF THE HEART

You need to talk to yourself more!

While some people consider it a sign of madness, others suggest they're always glad to have a conversation with a sensible person. As you seek to follow Jesus, your inner conversations will form the bedrock upon which you build the "House of God" in your life.

The Psalmist wasn't ashamed to talk to himself. "Why so downcast oh my soul?" he ponders, "put your trust in God." He returns to the thought again as he reflects on his difficult circumstance, but mentions in passing that he has found comfort in God's song. (This theme will occur again later in the chapter. The idea of God singing ... To quote the popular phrase of today: How great would that be!)[1]

Beyond religious observance, ethical passion, personal holiness, and all the other phrases that capture something of what following Jesus is believed to mean, the role of the inner life looms large. This inner life, convention has it, is nurtured by our daily quiet time, which may involve Bible reading and prayer. For many however, a quiet time is not something that stimulates them. They would prefer a noisy time, singing songs and praying out loud. They're not so sure about just reading the Bible. If you simply read it, how much will you remember?

To compound things, they may be tortured by the idea that if they're not having a twenty-minute session with God every day, then they're not a very good Christian. A good thing has become a bad thing for them as they struggle with another performance-oriented task.

So, how can we cultivate the habits of the heart that will enable us to give God's love away? How can we open up the ears and eyes of our heart so that God can teach us from His word, from His conversation with us by means of the Holy Spirit, and from His fingerprints in the natural world? This is our sixth learning path: revelation from God.

Here's a clue. It's hard to be passionate about someone you feel will always think you are inadequate. If you view God as someone who is perpetually angry with you, then the thought of praying to Him or studying His words will fill you with a mixture of obligation and reluctance, a confusion of emotions you would often rather avoid. Heart habits are easier to cultivate in a mind that fears God simply for His awesome majesty, creative power, and sheer indescribable virtue.

Heart habits may come more naturally when you're fascinated by God, curious about Jesus, and hungry for the character fruits of the Holy Spirit. Heart habits require choices and discipline. They are powerfully stimulated by curiosity, a desire to serve others and to show them something of Jesus. But perhaps we should examine the "why" of personal devotion before we plunge into something of the "how."

DIFFERENT PATTERNS

We are emotionally, mentally, and physically touched by the daily stimuli that touches our lives from the moment we wake until we sleep. A pleasant word from one person, a barbed comment from another. A beautiful sunset, a polluted and untidy yard. A hug or a kiss or an absence of affection. Our mood will be effected by the day to day realities of our lives.

The patterns of our thinking will be established as the result of a mixture of values, spoken and unspoken, the experiences of our lives, and our predisposition toward a self-centered view of life. The writer to the Romans calls us to give our lives over to Christ as a sacrifice and to be renewed in the patterns of our thinking. Our small and large habits of personal devotion are part of that renewing. We consciously reflect on our faith in order to re-order our thinking and re-stock the mind and heart with images, word pictures, words, and truths that will help us when we're internally talking our way through a life situation.[2]

HIDE THE WORD
The Psalmist loves the idea of hiding God's Word in our hearts and contends that it helps him to avoid sin. Jeremiah boasts of feasting on the Word of God and the joy and delight that ensued. The writer of Deuteronomy urges the people to have the Word of God near them, in their hearts and mouths so that they might obey it. A wise man's heart is said to guide his mouth so his lips might promote instruction.[3]

One of the reasons for reflecting on God's Word therefore is to ensure that the Word of God is near us. It will guard us, instruct us, and guide us by shaping the thought patterns, thought connections, and emotional backdrop of our lives.

THE INSTRUCTED TONGUE
But the wisdom of God isn't merely for our inner conversation. It's for the mundane and sublime moments of life and will often find literal expression in our conversation. One of the reasons for meditating on Scripture and talking to God in prayer relates to the content, quality, and tenor of what we communicate to others.

Sometimes our mere presence is enough, as people engage with the joys and travails of life. But sometimes we're the comforter or the truth-teller—the prophet or the pastor, with respect to their life situation. What are we to say in these situations if all we have to offer is common platitudes?

A foundational motive for being fluent in the wisdom of Scripture is a desire to bring words that heal or reveal. In the book of Isaiah, the prophet thanks God for "an instructed tongue that knows the word that sustains the weary."[4]

The wisdom of Proverbs also reminds us that the "lips of the righteous nourish many."[5] Savor that phrase for a moment. Your words could nourish people. Your encouragement could help them persevere. Your insight could steer them from danger. Your comfort could help them through their darkest hour. Your simple conversations could help shape their understanding of God, life, Jesus, church, the Holy Spirit, work, culture, or parenting.

If curiosity and a desire to serve stand alongside worship and reverence as part of the reasons for acts of personal devotion, what might those acts involve?

MEDITATING ON THE WORD

There are many ways to interact with Scripture. Some simply read it and respond to verses that "come alive" to them. Others will read a passage at normal speed, then read it a verse at a time, pausing to think about a phrase that strikes them. A question may be sparked, and a set of Bible reading notes or a commentary can give further insight.

Others listen on tape and perhaps watch on video, particularly when literacy is a problem. This would seem to reflect the experience of believers throughout the ages. They did not have ready access to the Bible and would rely on the reading skills of others or the dramatic re-telling by a gifted storyteller.

Others set themselves deliberate goals or commit themselves to a process that will cause them to reflect on the Scripture. How does this work?

I'm currently preparing the small group study notes for the cell groups in our church. We're preaching on the parables at present. Researching the notes has deepened my own understanding of Jesus' teaching methods and His use of story. It's also provocative.

One can view the story of the son who said he would help his father but didn't, and the one who said he wouldn't but did, as a warning to honor our fathers and keep our promises. But it's a biblical satire, a witty riposte by Jesus to the temple authorities who were questioning His authority to teach. He goes on to compare the reluctant son to the tax collectors and prostitutes who were following Jesus and John the Baptist, despite their unlikely status as workers for God. Think Michael Moore showing *Bowling For Columbine* at the Republican HQ of your state, or someone showing a pro-life video at a feminist convention, and you'll get a feel for the tension this story would have provoked.

The "deliberate goal" study strategy will also be helpful to some. I've committed myself to searching out books on the Gospels and the life, death, and resurrection of Jesus. I'm constantly interacting with Scripture as I read these books and use them for study and writing.

You can discover more about Scripture by following your passion. I've searched for books on thankfulness because I became fascinated with the use of thankfulness as a refrain in Colossians 3: 12-16. Thankfulness is a key to discipleship throughout Scripture. At other times, I've set out to find out about the role of smell in the Scripture, and another quest relates to finding out what the Bible says about sleep. Sometimes I just get fascinated by what a search at BibleGateway.com throws up. When researching the parable of the wise and foolish builders, I looked up foundation and discovered more than forty verses. These spoke to many different aspects of the security we find in God and made an excellent prayer outline.

PRAYING TOGETHER
Praying alone is clearly important. Jesus withdrew on several

occasions to pray alone, but much of the prayer of the Hebrew people was communal. They thanked God for their food and blessed Him for all manner of things. They gathered to eat on a Friday and included prayer and worship within their meal.

The different districts took turns in supplying volunteers for the temple. They would journey up for a week twice during the year, and special prayer activities would take place during that time back in their hometown.

Public prayers were held in the temple three times a day, and the disciples continued to attend these after the resurrection and ascension of Jesus. The book of Acts reminds us that they gathered daily. It was a prayer meeting that the miraculously set free Peter returned to.

It seems clear that personal piety wasn't confined to quiet rooms and could also find expression through communal worship. St. Thomas Crooke's Church in Sheffield, part of a tight-knit urban community and one of the five biggest churches in the U.K., has five meetings every day. They maintain a rhythm of prayer and reflection that can provide an oasis of spiritual refreshment for congregational members. The five services are not crowded and sometimes only attract a handful from the 2,000-plus congregation, but they represent an opportunity to focus and receive from God amidst the daily routines of life.

GATHERING

Scripture encourages believers to not give up meeting together. In this context, we can be spurred on toward love and good deeds. The Gospels and the book of Acts record more than thirty instances of the disciples talking together. We find that the disciples questioned Jesus about the meaning of His parables, their status in heaven, or how they might pray.[6]

Your heart will be fed by what you read. Your study of Scripture and your prayer with others and alone will all feed your soul. You'll discover truth in conversation and pray frequently in the course of the day as you thank God for food, pray for a child, comfort a friend, or respond to a request.

ALONE

There is clearly a need for us to sometimes be alone. We need to reflect as the psalmist did on his life situation.[7] We need to talk to God and discover the opportunity to focus. For some, that will mean literal quietness, but for others it will mean a walk through local park, or a praying and singing out loud time somewhere at home.

GETTING ON THE TIGHTROPE

It's time to get on the tightrope of faith. You must not wallow in spiritual apathy, too lazy to pray or read the Scripture, but you don't want to get locked into the legalism that sparks fear if you miss out one day. Ask the Holy Spirit to empower you with a holy curiosity, a desire for the words that will sustain the weary and a sense of the broadness of the ways God reveals Himself to us.

And while you're at it, sing more. Jesus was a singer. He sang Psalm 118 with the disciples as they celebrated the Passover. He loved the psalms and quoted them in response to those who criticized the children who were celebrating His coming.[8] The psalms were not confined to the temple or the synagogue and often used tunes associated with grape treading, hunting, or special festivals.

Paul and Silas sang as they whiled away the hours in prison. The book of Psalms urges us to sing in our beds and speaks of the comfort God's song brings at night.[9]

A song helps a truth remain memorable. Jesus used a poetic, singsong form of Aramaic for the Beatitudes section of the Sermon on the Mount. He started each line with a successive letter of the alphabet. If He came to Brooklyn today, He would probably rap the Word.

Songs leave a deposit of truth in our hearts and minds. Think about this one for a moment. It may have become popular with your parents' generation, but what does it say to us today about our Nike, Coca Cola, Fortune 500, McDonald's, Gucci, Chanel, life-as-a-brand culture? Would singing this song regularly, or others like it, renew the patterns of our thinking? Would one small habit of the heart make a huge difference?

I'D RATHER HAVE JESUS

Words: Rhea F. Miller, 1922
Music: George Beverly Shea, 1939

I'd rather have Jesus than silver or gold;
I'd rather be His than have riches untold:
I'd rather have Jesus than houses or lands.
I'd rather be led by His nail-pierced hand.

Than to be the king of a vast domain
Or be held in sin's dread sway.
I'd rather have Jesus than anything
This world affords today.
I'd rather have Jesus than men's applause;
I'd rather be faithful to His dear cause;
I'd rather have Jesus than worldwide fame.
I'd rather be true to His holy name.

Than to be the king of a vast domain
Or be held in sin's dread sway.
I'd rather have Jesus than anything
This world affords today.

He's fairer than lilies of rarest bloom;
He's sweeter than honey from out the comb;
He's all than my hungering spirit needs.
I'd rather have Jesus and let Him lead.

Than to be the king of a vast domain

Or be held in sin's dread sway.
I'd rather have Jesus than anything
This world affords today.

1. Psalm 42
2. Romans 12:2
3. Psalm 119:11; Jeremiah 15:16; Proverbs 16:23
4. Isaiah 50:4
5. Proverbs 10:21
6. Hebrews 10:23-25
7. Psalm 42
8. Matthew 21:16-17; Psalm 8:2.
9. Psalm 149:5, 42:8.

12

PURE JOY AND EARTHLY PLEASURE

Do you ever feel like you might be in God's waiting room? Does that gnawing impatience you sometimes feel when you're waiting to see a doctor or dentist who is running late consume you? Why do we have to stay in this horrible earth, full of these horrible sinful people? God loves us—why do we have to stay here and suffer with them?

If we've been raised around a certain type of church, we may even be tempted to despise our bodies, our senses, and our earthly existence. Wouldn't it be better if we were in heaven, or somewhere close, thinking pure thoughts and not feeling any nasty feelings?

This all sounds very spiritual, but it comes from ancient Greek philosophy, not from the Bible. Those body-wary Greek thinkers also persuaded many that rhetoric, or persuasive speaking, was the best way to communicate. Churches that are influenced by this view of life constantly worry about feelings, desires, and passions, and they celebrate preaching and talking above all else. Prayer and worship in this context is very verbal and undemonstrative.

The Bible and the life of Jesus, our record and example of God's dealing with humankind, paints another picture altogether, affirming all five bodily senses again and again as avenues for pleasure and delight in prayer, worship, and life.

Would you be surprised to learn that you worship a God who values smell, touch, taste, sight, and sound? A sensual God with a sensual son who wants sensual followers. (Sensual is not being used here in the exclusively sexual sense that some might relegate it to.) That sounds like an extreme claim, until you read the ordinary everyday detail of Scripture.

A PLEASING AROMA

Did you know that God loves the smell of roast lamb and the juniper bush that the priests often used on the altars? (Apologies to all those vegetarians reading, but it is in the Bible.) Next time you're reading the Levitical commands (as you do regularly I'm sure), check out how often God describes a sacrifice offered to Him as a "pleasing aroma" (thirty-nine to be precise).

God, it seems, loves the creation He made and savors the fragrant smells of it. At the heart of the 24-7 worship God encouraged in the tent of meeting (tabernacle) and the temple, we discover fragrant incense and anointing oil—the latter made from fragrant cinnamon, cane, and other aromatic elements. The Israelites were given a formula for it by God and were encouraged to keep that recipe exclusively for use in worship. Eleazar was set aside to look after this and given the skill of a perfumer. Part of the furniture of the worship area included an altar of incense.

It seems clear that the worship of God involved the whole person, the nose included. Careful preparation and the use of skill by those who supplied the materials were also important.

In case we think this is just an Old Testament concept not applicable to the New Testament Church, the gift of a pleasing aroma surfaces again in the life of Jesus. The oriental Kings who scoured Israel in search of Him presented Him with frankincense and myrrh. At a crucial point in the Gospels, a female follower of Jesus anoints Him with perfume from an alabaster box. The value of the ointment is estimated at 300 dinar at a time when the minimum wage of the day was about one dinar a day. Such senseless extravagance enraged Jesus' accountant Judas and may have been part of what led Him to turn against Jesus. It also affronted the religious people of the day. They believed that an unclean prostitute should not be touching a holy man and that He shouldn't have allowed it. But imagine the scent of that expensive perfume filling the house for many days afterward.

So, it will not only be words that speak in prayer, worship, and life. God wants the worship experience to engage all of our senses. Could your home, office, or church smell beautiful? Would that be wrong? Not according to the biblical account.

Sandalwood has been said to invoke a sense of well-being that in turn causes the brain to release serotonin, which calms and soothes. It seems we have been hard wired by the creator to enjoy and benefit from the smells He has created.[1]

JUST ONE TOUCH

Stepping through the door of a prayer room one day, I found a six-foot, two-inch actor, a man's man, prostrate on the floor, face down, his arms outstretched. His right hand grasping a crown of thorns, he was immersed in a prayer experience that reminded him afresh of the sacrifice made by Jesus and drew him toward thankfulness. Touch or the feeling of being touched is an important theme throughout the Scripture. It is often used to help people grasp a key biblical idea.

The prophet Isaiah uses the language of touch, warmth, and comfort to describe how much the Creator of the universe loves us: "He tends his flock like a shepherd, he gathers the lambs in his arms and carries them close to his heart."[2]

Sometimes touch could be an abrasive reminder of repentance. People would wear rough sackcloth and ashes as a sign of penance for rebellion against the wisdom of God and harm done to others. Touch was also part of the scandal of Jesus' life. The people of the day, particularly the Pharisees, were hoping for a Messiah. They believed that purity equaled holiness and that God would send a Messiah to a holy nation. Significant parts of that purity related to avoiding the touch of unclean people.

Jesus did not abide by this prohibition, which was enshrined in dozens of small laws added to the biblical injunctions. Jesus allowed Himself to be touched by a prostitute (stop a second and think—a prostitute) who washed His feet with her tears. He spent time in the company of people considered ritually unclean. He touched the sick and infirm—putting mud on the eyes of one blind man and taking the hand of a dead girl. This is not remarkable to us, but it would have shocked many at the time. Touch was an important part of Jesus' message. Without words, He signaled acceptance, reconciliation, and hope.

Jesus didn't need to reach out and touch the leper; He could have healed him with a word as He did on another occasion with ten lepers.[3] But this leper, like all his fellow sufferers, would have been viewed as profoundly unclean in the society of the day, banished to live outside the cities, told to stay six feet from others at all times. Lepers were expected to enter the synagogue first and to leave last, having occupied a special compartment while they were there.[4] Jesus knew what He was doing when He chose to touch this poor leper; He was well aware of the shock that would ripple through the crowd when He did. It also took place near the beginning of His ministry and was a sign of His unwillingness to be hemmed in by the traditions of man or the opinions of the powerful.

Jesus also allowed women to touch Him.[5] In the religious culture of the day, holy men avoided physical contact with any woman they didn't know because if they happened to be menstruating, they believed this might make the man ritually unclean. But when the woman with the constant hemorrhaging touched Jesus, instead she found herself healed.

Paul urged the early Christians to greet each other with a "holy kiss." Jesus washed the feet of His disciples. Christian experience without touch is sterile and less than biblical. Both the Old and New Testament encourage the "laying on of hands." In some cases, this was a sign of identification, in others, a signal of blessing and affirmation, and in still others, a symbol of authority conveyed to the person being prayed for.[6]

There has to be a role within our lives and the lives of the faith groups we belong to for touch and tactile sensation. I have helped organize several 24-7 prayer rooms. People book one-hour slots in a centrally located prayer room and discover new ways to pray as they try up to fifteen different prayer ideas. One prayer room idea that has touched people quite profoundly is one that involves nails. Huge nails the size of those that pierced Christ's hands on the cross are left near the start of the prayer journey within the room. Scripture verses remind people of the nature of Christ's sacrifice for mankind. Some people never get beyond the nails on their first visit to the room, so moved are they by the sheer physicality of this reminder of Christ's passion.

GLIMPSES OF GLORY

Count Zinzendorf, protector of the Moravians, an inspiration to the Methodists, and one of the founders of the modern missionary movement of the last 300 years, met with God one day as he gazed at a picture.

One of his defining moments, at the age of nineteen, came as he stood before a picture called "Ecce Home" in a Dusseldorf art gallery. The artist (Domenico Feti) had created a poignant image of a thorn-crowned Jesus and had inscribed in Latin at the foot of the picture the words: "This I have suffered for you, but what have you done for me?"

Zinzendorf, challenged to the core of his being, reflected that he had done little up to that point and asked God to remind him of Christ's suffering whenever he might be inclined to wander away from his first love.

This moment was to be a key one as he sought to discern the destiny God had for him. He had a God-encounter standing in front of a picture in an ordinary gallery, as had Moses before a burning bush.

We shouldn't be surprised—God loves beauty and creativity. He's always instructing people to make good things, and he has made for us a world that is visually spectacular. When we read that we are made in God's image, the only thing we know about God at that point is that He is an artist, a creator!

The first man in the Bible described as being filled with The Holy Spirit is not some great king or prophet. It is a craftsman called Bezalel, anointed by God to decorate the prayer room—the tabernacle.[7]

The temple, a centerpiece of our historical faith, was decorated with carvings of flowers and angels. There were free-standing sculptures of cherubim. Much of the temple was overlaid in gold.

This visual symbolism is reinforced by the descriptions of heaven in the book of Revelation. Revelation 4 uses the symbols of the harp and bowl to describe the singing and prayer of God's people. This chapter also describes a throne surrounded by a rainbow that resembles an emerald. The four horsemen of the apocalypse are described as having breastplates that are "fiery red, dark blue and yellow as sulphur." The Bible is not a monochrome text. It is full of color.

We can wear our prayers: The Jews were encouraged to wear symbols on their hands and foreheads to remind them of truth. They were also to write them on the doorframes of their houses and on the gates.[8] The priest Aaron carried two engraved stones embedded in his priestly costume. Joshua had the people from the tribes of Israel erect a monument of stones to serve as an eternal reminder of the provision of God. This monument would provoke questions from children and enable the parents to explain God's faithfulness.[9]

God doesn't want us worshiping objects or creating visual representations of others who claim to be deities.[10] A symbol becomes an idol as soon as it stops pointing to God. But God loves visual symbolism, as the short survey above suggests.

Remember that your faith is often symbolized by a cross or a small "Icthus" fish. Remember that an early prophet, indeed even the ancient prophets, used symbols such as belts, flying scrolls, and escape holes to visually alert the people (Agabus, Zechariah, and Ezekiel for the biblically curious).

Beauty, art, creativity, pleasing décor, symbolic drawings, and sculptures may all have their place in our personal visual landscape. Jesus brought another dimension to this visual feasting by speaking to the heart via the imagination. His parables took the profound and expressed it in terms of the mundane. A man once wrote that "the pictures are better on the radio." Could stories heard but not seen act on our internal visual creation ability and allow us to see God?

As we wrestle with the realities of worshiping a God we cannot see and whose earthly expression took place nearly two thousand years ago, we find in the parables of Jesus a chance to imagine God. Imagine for a moment you are a servant in the house of the father of the prodigal. You observe the nagging sorrow of the man who has lost a son and could not be blamed for harboring a deep sense of hurt and rejection. One day you see him start from his seat on the roof of the house and hurry out toward the path that leads away from the house.

There is an urgency about his step which forces him to hitch up his long robe and begin to run, an undignified thing for a man of his age to do. What would compel him to do that? Your eye turns to the horizon and your pulse quickens. That figure you see looks like his errant son. The father could wait in dignity and hurt anger to receive his apology, but he chooses to run to his rescue. He's not simply running to welcome him. He wants to signal to all in the local community that the son whose transfer of wealth from that area must have caused hardship to many is welcome and that he is to suffer no harm.

Our God, who calls His people back to Himself and makes promises to them via five Old Testament covenants, can be visualized as this passionate father who runs to the rescue of the son who turned his heart toward home.

O TASTE AND SEE

The Bible encourages us not to be gluttons or to idolize God's good gift of food. But it also seems to revel in feasting as well as fasting. Isaiah 25:6 promises deliverance for the people and a feast of rich food—the best of meats and the finest of wines. The words of God are described as being "sweeter than honey to my mouth."[11]

This may refer to the practice of teaching children the Hebrew alphabet by smearing the slate containing the characters with honey and allowing the children to lick the honey out of the letters. This ceremony was associated with their first formal lessons at the age of five and was part of the Shauvot festival.[12]

The Passover, the foundational liturgical meal of the Jewish faith, is laden with symbolism. Part of the meal included bitter herbs, symbolic of the coarse wild vegetables snatched by the fugitives at the roadside as they pushed on, further and further away from the oppressor. The wine represented the joy of emancipation, the intoxication of gratitude from a people escaping from the daily indignities of being slaves. Jesus affirmed the taste symbolism of the meal but concentrated on the bread and the wine, symbols of His body and blood.

The Psalmist urges worshipers to "taste and see that the Lord is good."[13] Jesus embraced the tradition of perceiving something of history and identity via the realm of taste.

HEARING FROM GOD, TALKING TO GOD

Words carry ideas, emotions, and much else. The Bible is one long conversation between God and humanity, recorded for our benefit. No one needs persuading that speaking to God is necessary, and our default communication will be words, spoken out loud or processed internally.

Jesus was a craftsman of words. Consider the Sermon on the Mount and particularly the Beatitudes. Translate it back into the original Aramaic and each sentence starts with a fresh letter from the alphabet. Jesus used an acrostic to help people remember His message. The whole speech has a sing-song quality and would lend itself to a pumping bass-driven hip-hop song. (Read that again. I've suggested that Jesus was a first century rapper.)

You can't help but feel there was some irony in calling Simon by a new name—Peter—when that word meant "rock," and Peter was the most volatile of all the disciples. Jesus is fond of the slightly absurd image too. He warns that a rich man will struggle to enter heaven in the same way that a camel would struggle to get through the eye of a needle.

Jesus was the human expression of a God who was known by His actions and often described in terms from everyday life, rather than from the pages of the philosophers' writings.

Brad H. Young talks of a God who "lays the foundations of the earth and shuts the seas with doors, who seeks an unfaithful people with the longing of a rejected lover and remembers a people with a mother's love. The biblical God speaks through images that touch hidden depths of human experience and cover the whole gamut of human emotions."[14]

Our words may be but a mere shadow of the reality of who He is, but they are one of the windows we have into the mystery of the divine.

To be a follower of Jesus is to be one who is in love with the life that is possible for us to have. We are living in an earth that was spoken of as being good six times by the Creator who was speaking it into being. We are made in His image and are to enjoy His creation. We are to know only one divide—that between idolatry and worship. Idolatry will lead us to seek sexual gratification wherever we might find it. Idolatry will be a route to a heart that values the acquisition of goods above honesty and respect for the others. Idolatry will take us on a path to gluttony. Idolatry will cause us to offer our lives to other deities and beliefs.

Worship will see our meals as a place of welcome, connection, and communion. Worship will perceive sexual joy within a covenant commitment as a gift from God, celebrated in the erotic and sensual imagery of the Song of Songs. Worship will see the earth as a tabernacle where our worship will be lived out as the overflow of a thankful heart.[15] Worship will have a place for feelings and the five senses. Worship will enjoy the earth, neither demonizing it nor worshiping aspects of it.

Worship will help us grasp the wisdom that enables us to avoid the seductions of this world's systems of thought. We'll live in that paradoxical state where we understand we are to love not the world, but also to revel in the fact that the earth is the Lord's and everything it.[16]

To those who are pure, everything is pure.[17]

Enjoy following Jesus.

---

1. "Inhale and Hearty," *Financial Times*, September 7, 2003.
2. Isaiah 40:11
3. Matthew 8:3
4. A. Edersheim, *Jesus the Messiah* (Hendrickson Publishers).
5. Matthew 9:20-22
6. Leviticus 8:14; Genesis 48:13-20; Acts 8:18
7. Exodus 35:30-31
8. Deuteronomy 6:4-8
9. Joshua 4
10. Exodus 20:4-6

11. Psalm 119:103

12. Strassfeld, Michael. *The Jewish Holidays: A Guided Commentary* (New York: Harper & Row Publishers, 1985).

13. Psalm 34:8

14. Brad H. Young, *The Parables* (Hendrickson Publishers). References Job 38:4,8; Hosea 2; Isaiah 49:14-15

15. Colossians 3:12-20

16. 1 John 2:15; Psalm 24:1

17. Titus 1:15

13

LIVING IN GRACELAND

Read your Bible/ pray every day/ if you want to grow. The melody is buried deep inside my mind. The sentiment even deeper. It's hard to fault the logic. If God is our Father, we should talk to Him regularly, and as the Bible is the record of His work, why wouldn't we keep that near the forefront of our minds?

It's worrying though. What if I miss a day? Does this mean I'm not committed? What if I don't understand the Bible—does this mean I'm spiritually insensitive? What if I struggle to pray—does this mean I'm hard-hearted?

Guilt. It's a good handbrake, but a poor steering wheel. But far too often we aim it at people as if it were a gun, loaded with truth. But it can destroy rather than build up.

Who is going to feed the hungry?
Who is going to share their faith today?
Who is going to pray for the lost?
Who is going to ask God for a purer thought life?
Who is going to give sacrificially to help us change the world?

Are we up to it? Can we last the spiritual pace and finish the race?

No.

We can't, and for many of us, the pain of trying can become too much. Perhaps you're like me. I was twenty-five, and I had graduated from Bible college. I was pursuing a career in the music industry and I was miserable. There was this nagging sense of failure. I was riddled with guilt. My prayer life, my thought life, everything. How could God use me?

It's not as if I was alone. Take Elvis Presley for a start. Steeped in Christianity, paranoid about upsetting his God-fearing mother. Torn between pleasure and guilt. Romancing Priscilla and trying to stay a technical virgin.

Marilyn Manson, the tortured soul who scandalized so many with this androgenous appearance and open mockery of Christianity, wrestled with faith in his early years and felt trapped in a "never-ending sin-and-repent cycle that you can't escape from." He said he felt guilty for being human.[1]

Tori Amos comments that she believes the faith of her formative years taught her that she was "unworthy and incapable." What I'm trying to inspire in my work is that we are capable. Tori captures her anger in the lyric to one of her best known songs, "Crucify": *Nothing I do is good enough for you.*[2]

Not everyone becomes totally distressed about rules and boundaries. Punk pop princess Avril Lavigne reflecting on her Christian upbringing comments, "That's a good way to bring up your kid, because if you let your kid do everything—go to parties, get trashed really young and get out of control—she's gonna get taken advantage of and she won't get taught that having sex with tons of boys is a bad thing."[3]

It might be suggested that whining about legalism is convenient for the terminally rebellious, who are anxious to avoid responsibility of their own destructive behavior. Sometimes hearing words of our own pained prodigals should provoke us to examine the way we communicate our faith, and the central theme of Christ's death on the cross.

But even as we grapple with the realities of that question, we have to also be aware that not everyone is simply a victim of the imperfection of others. We can't take seriously the reality of following Jesus without grasping the nettle of sin and evil. However keen we are to emphasize a God of love, a grace-filled faith, and a community of acceptance, we need a realistic view of human nature, or we'll simply be making soothing noises in the midst of emotional and physical anarchy.

THE ROOT OF THE PROBLEM

What, then, is the view of sin that many of us have? If you grew up in a certain kind of household, you might find your peers were going off to watch Disney films you were not allowed to see.

If eventually a television was permitted and your parents returned home after you on a Sunday, they might feel the television to ensure you hadn't been watching. Dancing was taboo (despite the energetic encouragements of Psalm 149). Secular entertainment was similarly dismissed as the work of heathen minds; playing cards were the devil's instrument and alcohol his poison.

Your faith was hemmed in by extra-biblical boundaries that helped you remain on the straight and narrow. You were such a degenerate, whatever your faith status, that you needed this unspoken control to keep you pure.

Jesus faced the same issues in his time. The core down-to-earth wisdom of the Law books and wisdom literature of the Old Testament had been supplemented by hundreds of other regulations—a fence built around the commands of God to help you to keep them. The idea that you shouldn't work on the Sabbath was absolutized and meant that you shouldn't heal on that day or rescue animals from a ditch.

In time, the keeping of these regulations becomes the measure of your holiness. But there was a price to pay. Heartfelt goodness could become supplanted by keeping- the-rules goodness, and become a mere observance rather than a choice to and bear God's image within creation.

When this mind-set is pervasive, what emerges onto the cinema screen of the Christian mind is a propaganda film about God. The deceiving script is written on people's hearts. God is angry, you are worthless, life is a struggle. The story may be familiar, but this judicial, forensic God who examines our every action and finds us lacking doesn't motivate us to relationship, merely to rule-keeping.

Holiness then becomes a sin management issue. How can I stop myself from sinning? How can I control my environment so I remain pure? What self-discipline can I practice that will keep me holy?

Hear me at this point. There are times when we have to say no to magazines, television programs, literature, and even friendships where a celebration of rebellion is the main agenda. The problem of legalism doesn't arise when we decide from personal conviction to place boundaries around our own hearts and minds. The problem arises when a major part of the Christian discourse we hear majors on our failings, formulas for holiness, and the anger of God. Profound truths become distorted half-truths because they are viewed in isolation from the bigger picture of God's will and purpose for us here on the earth.

This was the problem the prophets addressed as they spoke to the Israelites. A nation had come to place their faith in sacrifices as a means of appeasing God. Symbols of the cost of repentance and sorrow became an attempt to please God.

The prophet Amos warns that God despises their religious feasts. "Away with the noise of your songs. I will not listen to the music of your harps." God is aware that their idolatry is drawing them from a faith that reflects His love. He calls them to "let justice roll on like a river, righteousness like a never failing stream."[4]

But it was not just the Old Testament prophets who sounded this note. If we are wary of rules and law as a means to salvation, we are in good company. The apostle Paul warned us that the law provoked our conscience but could not in itself reconcile us to God.[5] Our good acts do not earn us reconciliation with God, but they are an expression of a renewed heart and a changed mind, good works that God has prepared in advance for us to do.[6]

Our friendship with God comes about through our faith in God. This enables us to claim forgiveness for the wrong that we have done and begin to understand the way of life that the law encourages, not the mere written down injunctions.

WHATEVER HAPPENED TO SIN?

How then are we to understand sin and the nature of our own hearts? At the root of it all is the concepts of worship and idolatry, relational living or a self-centered life.

God has created a place of wonder, awe, and beauty for us to live in. He has revealed to us the wisdom that will allow us to provide the best environments for our communities to enjoy God and live with one another within structures built on trust. At the heart of The Ten Commandments is relational justice. We are not to steal, kill, or seek sexual satisfaction outside of our marriages. We are to look after the elderly and be wary of placing our faith in objects, whether that be a religious belief or simply belief that acquisition will make us happy (Exodus 20).

God's rules and boundaries are the heartbeat of a value system that will ensure that humanity can live at peace within His creation. God has provided them because we have an impulse toward personal satisfaction and the worship of His creation, rather than thankfulness toward the Creator.

We take His good gift of food, to be enjoyed even when we

gather with Him to eat fine meats and drink aged wines, and become gluttons.[7]

We take His good gift of sex, celebrated in the erotic love poetry of Song of Songs, and turn it into an idolatry of the orgasm rather than a celebration of intimacy.

We take the beautiful things of His creation and turn them into objects of worship, or use the creative gifts He gives us as a means of personal aggrandizement.

So for us, the division is not between sacred and secular; it's between a life of worship orientated toward God and fellow humanity or a life of idolatry with self at the center.

Sin is an affront to God, not merely because of the statement of independence inherent in rejecting God's boundaries, but because of the anguish it brings to the lives of others. God's displeasure with sin is significantly related to His empathy with the victim and His awareness of the pain that trickles out throughout society when trust disappears and violation becomes the norm.

Not sinning heals the fabric of society; it restores trust; it renews hope. The choice to do good often undermines the impulse to sin as people begin to live their lives according to their values, not their feelings. God does get angry with sin, but as we will discover now, He is slow to anger, and His anger is related to the desire for justice that flows from His character.

DISCOVERING A GRACIOUS GOD

There are four different strands of thought about God and Jesus that will help us to discover what grace means for us. But first, what is our basic understanding of grace?

In pure dictionary terms grace, is often understood as unmerited favor. As Christians we believe that it is possible to be restored to relationship with God, despite our rebellious behavior and because God has decided to forgive us.

We are only required to make a covenant with Him. This involves us in acknowledging that He rose from the dead and in being willing to confess with our mouths that He is Lord, thereby signifying our willingness to serve Him. We are also called to confess our wrongdoing so the one who is "faithful and just" can forgive our sin and purify us from our past (1 John 1:9). The twin acts of confessing and seeking forgiveness both signify a decision of the will and an orientation of the heart. They are not the acts of someone seeking to win God's favor with good behavior, but are the expression of a surrendered heart thankful for God's mercy. They are the acts of someone who wants to re-orient their life.[8]

This is grounded in our understanding of the Father heart of God, which we discover both in the Old Testament and in the life of Jesus.

JESUS THE KING OF GRACE

Jesus exhibited unmerited favor to the diverse people He met. He opened His public ministry with the proclamation that He had come to declare the year of the Lord's favor. We see grace at work in His human interactions and in His willingness to give His life on the cross.

THE GRACE-FILLED LIFE

Jesus made a point of reaching out to those considered to be beyond the reach of grace at that moment in their lives.

Three incidents capture this. Jesus was returning to Galilee via Samaria. The Jews and the Samaritans viewed each other with mutual hostility. Jesus rested at Jacob's well while the disciples went to buy food. He asked a woman who came to the well for a drink. They talked of the water that would give eternal life, and then Jesus lead her into a dialogue in which He revealed He is aware that she has had several husbands. The dialogue continues, and many from the town come to see and hear the prophet who claims to be the Messiah.

It seemed remarkable that Jesus would extend His message to

the Samaritans, but the very fact that He engaged the woman in conversation at all was a spiritual statement of gracious intent.

Jesus extended this "grace before warning approach" on many occasions. He invited Himself to the home of the despised Zacchaeus and allowed a woman regarded by many as a prostitute to wash His feet with her tears and bathe them in perfume from her alabaster box.

But there was no cheap grace with Jesus. He was calling people to the values of a kingdom, but the invitations were not being delivered to the usual privileged addresses. The story of the prodigal son roots this picture of God's grace expressed through Jesus into the love of a heavenly Father.

There are several different metaphors or word pictures that express the meaning of the cross and speak to us of God's grace.

REDEEMER

The redeemer was the one who paid the ransom for someone who had been captured in a war. The ordinary man and woman was a slave to sin and rebellion, their lives dictated by the ruler of this earth. Christ came to give His life as a ransom for many. A price was paid in the blood Christ shed on the cross. The shame of being crucified was like a curse, but Christ nevertheless suffered all of this. God became man in Christ Jesus and suffered the pain and indignity of the cross so the power of the devil in the earth might be defeated and so the punishment sin deserved might be taken by Jesus Himself.[13]

SUBSTITUTE OR SACRIFICE

Jesus is spoken of as the slain lamb of God, whose precious blood takes away the sin of the world. The lamb given in sacrifice was to be spotless, meaning that the sacrifice cost the repentant one something. This cost was a token of their sorrow.[14]

COVENANT

Blood was also used in the sacrifices associated with covenant making. The blood shed by Christ signified the purifying that would come with the new covenant commitment between God and man because of Jesus.[15]

The biblical covenants were expressions of a loving Father God who was slow to anger and swift to bless, compassionate and gracious. God through the covenants expressed a love that could not be described adequately using metaphors of earth, sea, and sky. This same God is willing to remove our transgressions and put them as far as the "east is from the west." This same gracious Father sent His Son who didn't treat His people "as their sins deserved or repay them according to their iniquity."[16]

The covenants show us a God of the second chance who promised Israel the following:

The Noah Covenant: no more earth shaking floods.
The Abrahamic Covenant: descendants without number.
The Mosaic Covenant: a law to guide their ways.
The Davidic Covenant: the establishment of an eternal throne.
The New Covenant: truth written on humanity's hearts.

CHRIST THE VICTOR

Jesus came to the earth to confront the powers of darkness. These spiritual beings and forces combined with the rebellion of individuals to create systematic sinfulness that would often desecrate and destroy all aspects of creation.

Jesus' compassion, Jesus' miracles of healing and deliverance and His triumph over death through the resurrection disarmed these powers and authorities. Jesus set free a woman whom Satan had kept bound for eighteen years, calmed storms, and sent legions of demons from Gadarene demoniac.[17]

All the pictures presented to us with respect to Christ's work on the cross speak of a God who wishes to heal and restore, reconnect and make whole. We discover a God whose character is expressed in:

The patience of the covenant-making God.
The sacrifice of the God who redeems.
The self-giving of the God who takes the punishment our
rebellion deserves.
The rescuing God who comes to deliver people from the enemy
that seeks to compound their own rebellion.

We find seventy-four references in the Old Testament to the
"hesed" of God. This Hebrew word reflects the loving kindness
or mercy of God and carries the core idea of His faithfulness and
commitment to His promises. It expresses the triumphant promise
of Psalm 136, which details the historical commitment of God to
Israel throughout history and weaves this around the refrain, "His
love endures forever."

As you seek to follow Jesus, you will need to seize the grace of
God and His enduring love. Your life will be different as a result,
but it will never be perfect. You will need to believe the God who
forgave the adulterous David, the lying Abraham, the timid Moses,
the tempestuous Peter, and the murderous Saul of Tarsus will
forgive you.

Christ's death has conferred on you an external cleanness in the
sight of God. Even as you seek to serve God, you'll find the bonds
of past mind-sets and actions will be loosened.[18]

If your service is rooted in the joy of knowing the Creator, a
passion for the work of His Son, and a gratitude for the support
and enabling of the Holy Spirit, then you'll find you're at home in
Grace Land. You will have received the gift of salvation and find
yourself living a purposeful life of thankful response.

Following Jesus can be a joy when you're sheltering under the
cloak of grace.

1. Beliefnet.com
2. John Everson, "Tight Socks and Feminist Freedom," *Illinois Entertainer Magazine* August, 1994.
3. *Rolling Stone,* 2003
4. Amos 5:23-25
5. Romans 3:20
6. Ephesians 2:8-9, 10
7. Isaiah 25
8. I John 1:9; Romans 10:9
9. John 4
10. John 8:1-11
11. Luke 15:11-31
12. Isaiah 62
13. John 8:34; Mark 10:45
14. John 1:29
15. Hebrews 9:14-28
16. Psalm 103
17. Colossians 2:15
18. Hebrews 9:13-14

14

WISE UP

It was that time of year again. The youth group was about to be subjected to the twice a year lecture on sex.

This would usually take one of two forms. One: Staid but affable old missionary couple urges us to keep ourselves pure, observes the don't-sit-closer-than-six-inches rule, and saving kissing for the latter part of your engagement or marriage preferably. The youth group switched off quite early as you can perhaps imagine, and tried to stifle their mirth at the thought of this particular couple in a clinch.

Two: A twenty-minute lecture about the possibility of damage to our bodies (sexually transmitted disease), our emotions and those of others, and the possibility of pregnancy and loss of reputation. All true up to a point, but built on the mixed foundation of pragmatism and guilt. God will be offended; you might get hurt. Don't do it.

It was sound bite sex advice built around sin management rather than transformed thinking. It either seemed starkly out of touch with our reality or simply not enough.

There were at least three things missing in the little narratives we were given to guide us on our way. Nobody told us sex could be really good and the Bible celebrated it within the context of covenant and commitment. There was this overarching feeling that it was dirty.

Nobody talked to us in real depth about emotions, idealism, and romance and how our handling of our relationships might shape the self-worth and identity of the person we might be dating, particularly if the relationship was full of early romance and passion and then faded away into disagreement and a parting of the ways.

There was also little talk of the biblical idea of covenant. Covenant is a commitment that involves promises. God promised Noah that there would be no more worldwide floods. He promised Abraham that his descendants would be numerous. He promised David that his heritage would be sustained forever. Promise and commitment are the ideas that underpin our marriage ceremonies and are the bedrock notions that sustain us through the disagreements.

We heard nothing about those times when idealism has waned, and alongside the delightful, we see the flaws in the character of the one we've given our heart away to. We only heard about abstinence. It wasn't bad advice. It just wasn't enough.

The discipleship model held out to us was the best people knew. But in the area of sexuality and in many other aspects of life, it was built on guilt and willpower. It didn't seem to be built on a transformation in the way we thought. We were not being invited to countercultural patterns of thought.[1] Other than texts about fornication, we were not being invited to form a perspective shaped by the ancient, God-breathed wisdom of Scripture.

How can we help each other live the life that reflects the wholeness God has gifted us through Christ? How can we enjoy the task set before us rather than merely endure it?

How can we give an answer to that nagging voice that asks why? The voice that touches our guilt nerve because it feels like we're questioning God. The voice that sparks a sense of shame because we're not simply obedient.

We need to stop feeling guilty about that voice. To deny those questions is to invite ourselves to a blind unthinking faith. This is not the faith of the Bible, nor does it value the rich depths of Scripture and its ability to speak a response to our unspoken questions and thinking out-loud moments.

We need to wise up in a generation that often just wants to tune out or check the boxes of a handy formula.

WALKING THE LINE

As we seek to grasp what it means to be wise, we're going to have to grasp once again the nettle of paradox. God wants to speak to our minds and our hearts.

We live in a culture, both within the Church and often in wider society, that can often dismiss the mind and exalt feelings.

I sat in church one Sunday as the preacher denigrated those caught up in intellectual pursuits and theology. "I know a little Greek," he told the congregation, "he runs the delicatessen down our street."

In our wider culture, the ideas of postmodernism deny the truth claims of any ideology. The modern idea that the human mind could work out everything is denied, and we are encouraged to simply find something that works for us and perhaps not worry about its truth claims. Christians must now question postmodernism because it allows for no absolutes, no boundaries, and no standards for society.

Christians questioned modernism because of its view that the mind, and particularly the sciences, could answer every question and would ultimately expose Christian orthodoxy as a superstitious deceit. We reacted to the arrogance of the claim that the finite mind could understand the infinite. We questioned whether science really wanted to consider all the evidence in debates over evolution or genetics or the nature of humanity.

We neither want to elevate the mind or dismiss it. Our minds are God's gift to us. They are fallible and fallen as a result of our rebellion against God, but they are capable of being renewed.

It's vital that they are. If they're not, the super-spiritual move into the vacuum and torture us all with comments based on their feelings. Have you ever been in a debate with someone about Christian contemporary music? A familiar argument from the past decades related to that dread sentence, "My spirit witnesses against this incursion of the world into the Church."

What was happening here was that people's understandable revulsion at the excesses of rock culture was being transferred onto a group of people who were making a similar sound. One short sentence was loaded with prior assumptions.

Was their feeling from God or simply an expression of their own cultural prejudice? What are the criteria by which we reflect on culture?

• Broad biblical principle or our own emotional reaction?

• Who created music in the first place, and in what way can it be said to be worldly? God created it, and it can be used for worship or idolatry depending on the intent of those making it. Neither the devil or the world own any music form. We are not "using the methods of the world." They are abusing the gift of God.

• How should we evaluate the intent of the artist or the nature of the music or the lyrics? We need objective reasons for praising or critiqueing popular culture. This will help us be reflective when we respond to it. People will not be swayed by our

subjective feeling. Paul had evaluated the religions of Athens
when he stood on Mars Hill and spoke of their unknown
god and their worship songs to Zeus. He spoke to them
about a religious reality that lay beyond these mere shadows and
distortions of the Almighty. People will listen if we make an
effort to be aware.

• How much is contemporary music in debt to the Church,
which gave many of its practitioners, both black and white, their
first musical experiences? Did Luther, Wesley, and General
Booth borrow the popular tunes of the day to create the
traditional hymnody that we now deem respectable? Did the
contemporary music of the '60s contain songs that had been
taken from the Church ("Stand By Me"; "Turn, Turn, Turn")?
Where did Lifehouse, Avril Lavigne, U2, Norah Jones, Sheryl
Crow, Depeche Mode, Whitney Houston, Creed, and P.O.D.
learn the melodic and harmonic skills that have made them
some of the biggest stars in the world? They learned them in
church. Trying to figure out who is taking from whom is a bit
like asking what came first, the chicken or the egg.

• Do they get the same witness about Handel's Messiah, which
scandalized the Church authorities of the time when it was first
performed in a theater?

The dubious theology of some is given credence by an appeal
to special divine revelation. The logic of these dubious claims
only troubles people because they know there is a dash of truth
in there somewhere. We can't just blindly mimic mainstream
culture without ensuring that we are bringing a whole new set of
meanings to that art form or music. But leavening poor theology
with a little bit of truth doesn't make it any less an error. By the
same token, stopping to think about how music has been used in
the Bible and throughout Church history will enable us to use it
with wisdom.

I do believe however that there is such a thing as the witness of
the Spirit—a sense of affirmation or foreboding about certain

situations, places, or people. Whenever I feel it I start to think what would make this feeling make sense? What concrete facts can I gather to back up my intuition? I test my feeling. I weigh what I've felt. The Bible encourages us to weigh the prophetic word and to take advice from others when we receive it.[2]

But some who talk of their inner witness use their feelings in an authoritarian way. They are not ready to submit their feelings to the test. They use their feelings as a blunt tool to bludgeon you into seeing their perspective. They baptize every whim or thought with the phrase, "God told me."

This type of person values the Spirit above everything else. Events that appear supernatural are valued above the ordinary and mundane. "God is Spirit" is misquoted frequently to back up their assertions. For these people guidance often comes before obedience, miracles before perseverance. God becomes a majestic fortune teller, eager to disperse prophetic nuggets to guide them every step of the way.

As someone who values discernment of spirits, prophetic utterance, and the possibility of the miraculous, I don't want to see them discredited because they have been trivialized by those who would claim their every emotion is a sign from God.

Christians are not alone in using their feelings as the foundation of their decision-making. Non-Christians may also base their lives around their feelings. Every decision becomes centered on their own personal emotional management. Is this marriage good for me? Would I enjoy sex with this married man or woman? What will make me happy? Why should I tolerate anything less than what I perceive to be perfection? Would I feel better after cosmetic surgery? What will make me attractive to others?

LET'S GET BIBLICAL
Hebrew thought doesn't divide our humanness up. It values the mind, body, and Spirit. The Scripture urges us to love the Lord our God with all our heart and soul, mind and strength.[3]

The book of Proverbs reminds us that a cheerful heart is good medicine but a crushed spirit dries up the bones.[4] The Bible is a very sensual book, talking often in word pictures that reflect the use of all our five senses in understanding and perceiving God's world. God has ordained that all of our humanity is involved in the understanding and expression of our spirituality.

Perhaps you've been absorbed in a passive, fatalistic theology and you can't quite see the role of the mind and wisdom. You've been told to "let go and let God" or urged to stop trying to "follow God in your own strength because spiritual change is all about God and the work of the Holy Spirit."

I get a hollow feeling in my stomach when I hear people say, "I just want to thank God because I am useless/horrible/sinful and this change in my life is all a sovereign work of the spirit." It sounds as if God simply did a lobotomy on them and now they're His little robots. It sounds so spiritual, and the murmured amens echo round the sanctuary, but it's very hard to support biblically.

One of the best metaphors of spiritual change in the Bible relates to wrestling. Jacob wrestled with the angel of God. Peter was always jousting with Jesus as his headstrong views were tempered by the wisdom of the master. Job fenced with God and had to backtrack when reminded of the sheer awe of creation. The Psalmist is often found bemoaning his fate before conceding that he is going to persevere and trust God. None of this feels like "pray a prayer and you'll be spiritually mature in an instant because you are simply a channel for the Spirit" to me.

What it does suggest is that God gave us a mind, and we are to use it both in our relationship with God and as we begin to discern His will for humanity.

The Scripture seems quite clear.

The first eight verses of the book of Proverbs capture it well. We are urged to attain wisdom, to seek knowledge, and desire discretion. The wise are urged to add to all their learning. Throughout the Psalms and Proverbs, we are encouraged to remember God's teaching and to store it in our hearts.[5]

The key to how we can know what it means to be a disciple of Jesus is this: If our mind is infused with the prior belief that we are living in God's universe and that He has given us a book of guidance to help us understand it, our minds can be profitable tools. They will be shaped both by the Bible and the promptings of the Holy Spirit as we seek to worship God in "spirit and in truth." This worship is expressed through our lives, not merely through our songs and prayers.

Our minds can become the storehouses of wisdom.

THE SCOPE OF BIBLICAL WISDOM

As always, we will want to be wary of shrinking biblical wisdom to reflections on Church, marriage, and personal devotion.

With that in mind, the Bible can be a little shocking to the pious if you truly explore it, particularly the Old Testament. Deuteronomy is very down to earth and relates the Jubilee principle to the social and economic life of the nation. It has an underlying bias toward justice, with land lost by family members being returned to their descendents after fifty years.

But some of the detailed suggestions seem to relate to the mundane things of life. The Israelites were not to cut down fruit trees in war mix their seeds, or take a mother-bird.[6] They were to be concerned with the local ecology even in the midst of conflict. Elsewhere, God gives them guidance with respect to quarantine, body fluids, and sanitation.[7]

God, it seems, wanted the people of Israel to know the things He asked were not just His whimsical commands, but they had a rationale behind them. Other law codes existed among the other nations around the Middle East, but none offered reasons.

Here are some examples of God's rationale:

Free your slaves: They were to be released after six years as the master would have done well out of their service.

Don't bribe: It makes it difficult for even a wise man to think straight.

Punish perjurers: Otherwise people will simply lie in court.

Too many wives: The king is not to have many wives or his integrity will be threatened.

Cities of Refuge: These were to be a haven for people caught up in feuds but whose hearts were innocent.

Care for the local ecology: Soldiers were instructed to not use fruit trees for war purposes. This meant the restoration of personal and local stability would be quicker following war.[8]

This pattern of concern for the everyday is found throughout the Old Testament. The Song of Songs gives detailed erotic information for would-be Israelite lovers (although I would be cautious about a male reader telling his loved one that she has a neck like a gazelle, lest you be subject to an inquest on whether you are suggesting that she is fat/thin/look like an animal!). The book of Esther doesn't mention God. The book of Ruth has very few references to God. Both books seem to be about how one might live one's life in the light of God, but they don't talk about Him much.

The book of Proverbs is also full of wisdom for our 24/7 lives, not just the devotional aspects of our faith. The wisdom giver seems to chuckle at the buyer who downplays the product he's buying only to express his delight when the purchase is made.[9] The reader is encouraged to humility, especially in the presence of a ruler. He or she is also urged to be careful in all aspects of speech.[10] The New Testament comments on civil government, the care of widows, and divorce and re-marriage.[11]

CREATIONAL INTENT

At the core of all this wisdom teaching is a call to the people
to be aware of the creational intention of God. Looking to that
creational intent is a key to understanding much of what God has
asked us to do and why He asked us.

Let's take a look at what might seem like an obscure subject—
blood—and then look at how understanding the following four
principles might help us.

- What was God's creational intent?
- How did humankind's rebellion affect this?
- How has Christ's life, death, and resurrection changed our
  attitudes?
- What can we do now to help restore the wholeness that is at
  the heart of God's intent?

Creational—God's creational intent for blood was as a means of
giving life and carrying nutrients and many different types of
information around the body.[12]

Fall—The ancients were advised by God that the blood could
be a carrier of all types of disease, and that purity with respect to
the blood of animals was vital for their own health.[13] The fall, or
humanity's rebellion against God, also meant that the possibility
of sexual contact with multiple partners opened up the way for
infections to spread from person to person via the bloodstream.
Cervical cancer is more common in those who have had multiple
sexual liaisons. AIDS has spread in the gay community because of
the rectal tearing associated with anal intercourse. Blood-tinged
needles have spread it in the heroin using population.

Infections via the blood of animals are at the root of the BSE or
mad cow disease problems that have both infected humans and
done so much damage to European agriculture. Animals fed on
the crushed remains of other animals carry the disease into the

human food chain. It has also been suggested that the SARS virus which caused so much trauma in the far East in 2003 was derived from the eating of a certain type of cat. There are also those who believe that AIDS entered the human biological arena via the use of monkey related cells in the polio vaccine popular in medical circles during the '60s and '70s.

Biblical hygiene laws can be seen therefore as relevant to the realities of tribal health and not the mere foibles of a ritualistic society.

Redemption—The commitment to one partner of the opposite sex that has been the call of the Church since the time of Jesus radically reduces the spread of sexual disease. God through Christ and the Holy Spirit seeks to give us the reason, the motivation, and the empowerment to make that happen.

The application of a biblical perspective on animal husbandry and the vigorous pursuit of clearer policies in this area will be the mark of a prophetic Church which believes that violation of the creation order releases many unforeseen consequences.

Restoration—The Church will also want to apply these principles to all areas of life. The genetic engineering lobby in our society promises great good from their tinkering with the human genome. There is a growing awareness, however, that a gene represents potential behavior, not predictable behavior. A gene is influenced by many things, including the proteins carried to it via the blood stream. There is a level of complexity with respect to how the body works that should give us pause for thought before combining previously unrelated genes, particularly those from animals that may react in unpredictable ways with the human body.

It is possible to then apply this framework to other areas, such as sexuality.

Creation—Erotic love was to be both pleasurable and procreative.

Fall—People began to seek the pleasure while avoiding the consequence. Some societies practiced infanticide and abortion. Others offered children as sacrifices, this being a principle problem with the Baal worshippers of the Old Testament times.

Redemption—The metaphor of marriage is used by the biblical writers to describe the relationship between Christ and the Church. The Bible also echoes the themes of covenant, commitment, and trust. From this it follows that God honors marriage and that it can be modeled on the covenant relationships of God.

Restoration—The people involved a sexual relationship should be in covenant commitment because the fruit of their activity might be a child. The child needs many different levels of nurture, from feeding through to affection and on into social, educational, and spiritual nurture. The mother and father bring different skills, which complement each other and create a healthy climate for the growth of the child.

If we return now to our original question at the beginning of this chapter regarding how we might think wisely about sex, we begin to see a pattern emerging.

- We can enjoy it, but it has a context—covenant relationship.
- That covenant is needed because it has a consequence—children.
- Children need the security of stable two-parent relationships if they are to experience the full parenting experience.
- Monogamy also lessens the possibility of the violation of the blood/body fluids barrier that is the carrier for much disease.
- Understanding the importance of the blood may also help us think wisely about other key areas such as animal care, dietary choices, genetic engineering, and other contemporary issues.

Books could be written on small parts of this chapter. I trust it starts a process of thinking that will cause you to have both the mind of Christ and the wisdom of the patriarchs.

If you want to follow Jesus, you're going to have give Him your mind as well as your heart.

1. Romans 12:1-2
2. 1 Corinthians 14:29
3. Deuteronomy 6:5; Matthew 22:37
4. Proverbs 17:22
5. Proverbs 1:1-8
6. Deuteronomy 20:19, 22:19, 22:6
7. Deuteronomy 23
8. Deuteronomy 15:18, 16:19, 17:13, 17:17, 19:3-7, 20:19
9. Proverbs 20:14
10. Proverbs 25:6, 25;11
11. Acts 5; 1 Timothy 5:9; Romans 13
12. Leviticus 17:11
13. Genesis 9:4

15

THE FOOLISH THINGS

Jesus was an asylum seeker.

His earthly parents fled to Egypt to protect their child from the murderous Herod. Fearful that a child king might challenge his claim to reign, he ordered every child under the age of two killed.

The Savior of the universe knew what it meant to be part of a minority, a child far from home, living on the fringes of a society where attitudes to His presence may have been ambivalent at best, hostile at worst.

Jesus emerged from the fringes of society, the son of a carpenter, eventually raised in the unfashionable town of Nazareth. He collected together a group of marginal people and started a spiritual revolution that rumbles around the earth to this day.

God decided to use the foolish things of the world to confound the wise.[1] Perhaps we should examine what the wise might say to us today, and question once again whether God has some foolish people He wants to use in this generation.

Perhaps you equate foolishness with bizarre witnessing activities, or simply being resolutely different, simply to prove a point and feed your sense of spiritual martyrdom. I'll be a fool for Christ, you promise yourself.

I can feel my teeth grinding even now as I think of the poor humor, self-consciously wacky behavior, and general nonsense I've seen justified under the blanket covering of "being a fool for Christ." I'm searching for something a little deeper than that. What are those foolish things that confound the wise?

RIGHT TIME, WRONG CROWN

Jesus arrived at the right time, but wearing the wrong crown as far as many were concerned. A man of undoubted piety, possessed with miracle power and a razor sharp intellect, His wisdom was well received by the people, but He wouldn't play the power, purity, and revolution games in which the opinion formers wanted Him to indulge.

They had a certain expectation of how a messiah might look, sound, and behave. There were several pictures or themes in the Old Testament concerning the promised Messiah. One theme pictured a prophet like Moses, another spoke of a suffering servant, but many hoped for a king like David, a figure who would triumph militarily and drive out the Romans, thereby restoring the dignity of a subjugated race.[2]

The feeding of the five thousand sparked a messianic fervor in the people of Israel. Surely the promised prophet had arrived? They were eager to proclaim Him king, compelling Him if He was reluctant. Jesus fled to the hills. He had come as the suffering servant and was not about to be drawn into the nationalistic politics of His day.

Jesus' insistence on being the quiet king of hearts, rather than the violent king of battles, would earn Him a mocking crown of thorns. But for those with eyes to see and ears to hear, it was clear from the day angel choirs filled the wastelands with songs heard only by shepherds that this was a man like no other.

God had made it clear from His birth that Jesus was not going to court the wise, but would lift up the poor and disempowered from their lowly status and place them at the center of the salvation story.

IN THE COMPANY OF DONKEY DRIVERS

If the archangel Gabriel had been God's spin doctor, he would never had allowed him to announce the arrival of the Son of God to some heathen kings and a nomadic group of shepherds. What credibility would they have with the council of the Jews, the scribes and Pharisees, and indeed the ordinary man or woman in the dusty Galilean streets? Very little.

The distortions of pagan religion had nevertheless led the wise men to discover a king whose coming would be symbolized by the presence of a star. They were hardly credible witnesses in the minds of a religious establishment concerned with the purity of the faith and a rigorous observance of ceremonial law.

The shepherds were hardly any better. While God was fond of using the shepherd as a metaphor for His care and comfort, the ordinary shepherd got fairly bad press among the people of Jesus' day.[3]

Together with donkey drivers, tanners, sailors, and camel drivers, they were considered a despised group. Their occupation made them more vulnerable than most to the possibility of ritual uncleanness through contact with animal blood or fecal matter. Their need to be in the fields at night meant they weren't at home to protect their women and children. They grazed their flocks on other people's property and were therefore considered thieves. They appeared twice on a rabbinic list of proscribed trades.[4]

Why didn't God choose more credible witnesses? Because God was subverting the religious order of the day by sending a Son who would touch the lives of all in the nation. No one group could own Him.

A MOTLEY CRUE

Jesus' disciples didn't exactly read like a list of candidates for high office in a movement of cultural change.

It was a mark of the impact of His life and personality that He had such radically different characters walking the roads of Galilee, Judea, and Samaria with Him.

Let's take a short look at what we know about them:

MATTHEW—A TAX COLLECTOR

Jesus is known to have had many tax collectors among His followers.[5] Tax collectors fall into three groups: The leading ones were working actively with the Romans and were not acceptable in any way to the religious leaders of the day. Others who worked for them became quite well off, but were considered dishonest if they did. The final group were simply workers in a profession that left them poor and poorly regarded. Tax collectors were often rootless individuals desperate for work.

While other ordinary men and women who shared the tax collectors' will to survive may not have looked down on them, the tradesmen of the day viewed them with suspicion, and the rich and educated held them in contempt.

The religious were wary of them, particularly those who set a high standard of purity and did not welcome the potentially unclean and uninvited visiting them to levy tax. They were not liked by the rabbis who forbade the people to receive charity from the leading tax collectors and ranked them with heathens, harlots, and highwaymen in the listings they were fond of producing.

SIMON THE ZEALOT

How Simon felt about Matthew is open to speculation. The

Zealots had risen to fame in the early years of Jesus' life because of their refusal to pay financial tribute to a pagan emperor, on the grounds that was treason to God, the real King of Israel.

FISHERMEN

At least seven of Jesus' followers were fishermen (Peter, Andrew, Philip, James, John, Nathaniel, and Thomas). The people who caught the fish rarely benefited as much as those who handled it from then on. Many fishermen were part of partnerships in which the local tax authorities were the senior partners. Fishermen were not exactly near the top of the social ladder.

Nine out of twelve of His disciples were involved in tasks considered marginal or regarded with hostility. Jesus didn't recruit the obvious talent, despite His friendship with council members, such as Joseph of Arimathea and Nicodemus.

IN WORD AND IN DEED

Jesus had been announced to marginal despised people. He then recruited them to be His followers and embarked on a life of calculated kindness that undermined the unloving legalism of the day, even before He spoke a word.

Jesus habitually loved people. He talked to an immoral Samaritan women, despite the risk this posed to His reputation. He affirmed the faith of the centurion, the agent of an occupying force. He sent the woman caught in adultery on her way with no stinging rebuke, but a simple command to "go and sin no more."

But perhaps the most shocking incident concerned a chief tax collector—Zacchaeus. It's tempting to look at this incident through third millennium eyes. Jesus welcomed a tax collector. No one is fond of the IRS. Jesus cut across the prejudice of His day. The story has some power even at that level, but actually it's far more symbolic than we perhaps realize.

Picture the scene. Jesus is walking toward the town of Jericho. He's known to be a healer and can more than hold His own in a verbal joust with the wise and learned. He's a great storyteller, and there's always some excitement when He passes through.

Jericho is probably ready for some street entertainment. As Jesus approaches, the crowds are probably gathering, provoked by gossip from local traders who've heard from their contacts He's on the way.

As He draws near, different expectations ripple through the crowd. Perhaps the father of a blind child hopes his miracle will come today. Another reflects on the rumors he's heard about Jesus. Seems He may not be the liberating warrior that some had hoped for. A Pharisee hurries toward the main square, frowning as he ponders the stories circulating in this, the second most priestly city of the Jews. Jesus is claiming to be introducing the kingdom of God, but from all he's heard, it seems He's a glutton and a drunkard who mixes with publicans and sinners and breaks both venerable tradition and the Sabbath.

Elsewhere, a social outcast ponders how he can see the man of the hour, without drawing the notice of a crowd likely to be rude at best and hostile at worst. He hides himself in a tree and waits.

It could have been such an ordinary but extraordinary day. Jesus could have healed the sick, argued with the teachers of the law, and told the attentive crowd stories of a loving father who welcomed back his prodigal son or a shepherd who found his lost sheep.

To the warm delight of the crowd, He could have turned His gaze on the errant tax collector and reminded him that God would judge him for exploiting the poor. The words of Amos, Hosea, and Micah could have rung out. It would have been an exciting end to a great day.

But it was not to be. Jesus chose to scorn the scorn of thousands to win the heart of one.

He looked up and said, "Zacchaeus, come down immediately. I must stay at your house today." The crowd bristled. This man is unclean. This man robs us. This man consorts with the Romans. A crowd hoping for the benevolent favors of a miracle worker now channels that frustrated hope into an anger that Jesus would treat this man as an equal.

There would have been outrage in the crowd. The biggest anger would have been felt by the priests and religious people. To help people keep the law or the Torah, they had added over 300 additional laws. This would help create a pure nation, worthy of a liberating Messiah. Many of the additional rules concerned eating and food. Given Middle-Eastern hospitality customs, it was inconceivable that Jesus would visit the tax collector's house and not eat.

In one sentence, Jesus undermines the religious status quo of His day. It would have been deeply upsetting to the power brokers of popular religion to see this wise man, this healer, undermine their norms. It made Him a spiritual and political threat.

Zacchaeus indicates he will ensure in the future that he treats people fairly and that he will make restitution if necessary. Jesus welcomes him into the family of Abraham, proclaiming salvation had come to that house.

Knowing full well His words would be reported, Jesus finishes this provocative statement with the reason why He came: to seek and save the lost.[6]

Jesus maintained a steely distance from compromise with sin. He rebuked the temptation of Satan; He argued with the legalists of His day; He called ordinary men and women to repent and get ready to embrace the values of the kingdom. He warned us to avoid not just sin, but the emotional extremes that sparked it.

But all the while, He mixed freely with the impure, marginal, and lost.

In case people missed the message of His life and actions, He spelled it out in His parables and stories.

The selfish, materialistic prodigal son is welcomed home when his heart turns back toward the memories of care, security, and love. In the parable of the great banquet, the lame, the poor and the wretched are welcome to the meal, summoned from the streets and alleyways when the rich and the noble make their excuses and decline to attend.

Perhaps the most poignant statement of Jesus' care for the marginal comes in His reflection on the future in Matthew 25: 31-46. While one group stands before God and is banished to eternal punishment for neglecting the poor and needy, the other is welcomed in for being willing to feed Christ when He was hungry, clothe Him when He was naked, or visit Him when He was in prison.

The confused recipients of God's favor can't remember doing this, but they are told that whenever they did it, it was as if it had been done for Jesus.

Here is the heart of what we're journeying toward. Our conduct is not a duty, not a set of laws to be kept. But it is a means whereby we can worship, undertaking the good deeds God has prepared in advance for us to do. When we begin to think of life as an act of thankfulness, a giving away of God's love, our perspective changes.

In the book of Proverbs we are called to: Speak up for those who cannot speak for themselves, for the rights of all who are destitute. Speak up and judge fairly; defend the rights of the poor and needy.[7]

Jesus and all those who would follow Him are called to speak the truth with love to every sphere and sector of society. At the heart of Jesus' life we find counter-intuitive behavior, a mixing with the poor and the powerless. Jesus didn't seem to be pursuing some carefully thought through trickle-down theory of influence and change. He simply loved people and never let social convention or religious law stifle that.

CLUES FOR THE HERE AND NOW

When Jesus spoke to or ate with people deemed unworthy by others, He sent out powerful signals. Mundane behavior such as eating together spoke of acceptance, acceptance sparked trust, trust released hope, and hope sought salvation.

Author and speaker Ed Silvoso reminds us in Prayer Evangelism (Regal Books), that we often start our contact with non-Christians with verbal declarations of our faith. Offers of healing prayer may come next. Eventually we may ask them to share the everyday normality of a meal with us before we ask God to bring peace to their home and family.

Jesus' words to His disciples as He sends them out to prepare the way for Him are instructive. Consider the order in Luke 10:5-9.

"When you enter a house, first say, 'Peace to this house.' If a man of peace is there, your peace will rest on him; if not, it will return to you. Stay in that house, eating and drinking whatever they give you, for the worker deserves his wages. Do not move around from house to house. When you enter a town and are welcomed, eat what is set before you. Heal the sick who are there and tell them, 'The kingdom of God is near you.'"

Part of the challenge of this passage lies in the order in which Jesus suggests things be done.

Declare peace—This formed part of a common greeting at the time. But it could be much more than a mere verbal punctuation mark. It was a prayer. Does it provoke us about our tendency to pray "against" things when we begin to think about how to pray for our area, town, or street? Jesus is inviting us to invite Him to bring peace to that area. The mere announcement that God's peace is coming to that place is a form of spiritual warfare that drives away destructive forces that may have strongholds there.

Eat with people—Eating together allowed discussion, signified acceptance, and was a redemptive act in it own right when practiced by Jesus with the social outcasts of the day. It reminds us to be with people in the ordinary rhythms of their lives, building friendship and trust.

Pray for their healing—Jesus prayed for people to be healed. Some were deeply grateful and no doubt became part of His band of followers. Others, including nine lepers, expressed little thanks. In our culture, people seem ready to be prayed for, even if not all acknowledge the healer who might come to their aid. Healing prayer seemed to be a gateway for the message of Christ's life. It enabled trust to grow and readied people to hear the message of the kingdom.

Declare the Kingdom. The story is told of a concert in an American city, featuring a militantly anti-Christian band. Their fans sweltered in the sun as they waited for the doors to open. At one end of the street, a church group held up banners proclaiming that God hated gays. Further down the street, another church group, noting the plight of the line, made gallons of cold drinks and offered it to people as they waited. Hundreds of young adults had some of their caricatures of Christians—encouraged by the banner wavers—undone by a simple act of acceptance and help. A church group declared peace to the crowd and helped feed them. They were much more likely to get the opportunity to pray for their needs and declare the good news of Jesus' kingdom to them.

Jesus didn't send out His followers alone. They ventured into the wider world together. Jesus often met with those considered "sinners and publicans" in the company of several of His followers. We will not want to face some of the challenges of the culture we live in alone, but we will never change it by hiding in our castles and staging confrontational raids on the hearts of the lost via occasional street preaching or door knocking.

In towns and cities around the world, door knocking is starting to work again because its primary purpose is not to engineer a conversation, but to simply make contact, offer prayer, or convey information about church events or children's clubs. At first you are given seconds at the door, but in time, trust is built; people become your acquaintances and then your friends.

The message for us is this: Impersonal evangelism may leave the fingerprints of God on someone, but only the friendship that flows from genuine love for others will help this generation feel the embrace of God.

The challenge is this: Will we forever regard the not-yet-Christian as "them," objects of spiritual pity, rather than objects of God's love? Will we be their friends whether or not they make an immediate response to our talk of faith? Are we prepared to enjoy life together with them on shopping trips, in the bleachers of a sports stadium, or relaxed around a late summer barbecue? Are we willing to connect with non-Christians and dare to believe we can influence them for good, rather than them corrupting us? Do we believe He who is in us is greater than he that is in the world?[8]

As we consider matters of social justice, are we motivated by pity or compassion? Pity says, "I will help you because I feel guilty, or maybe because I feel superior." Compassion says, "I will help you because you're human, made in the image of God and worthy of dignity, friendship, and aid."

Jesus was colorblind, status-blind, and gender-blind. He didn't see the divisions we often see. He created a Church where there is neither Jew nor Greek, male nor female, slave nor free.[9]

Jesus did not come with mere words of wisdom before scurrying home to a spiritual fortress. He lived among and ate with the ordinary people of His day. He was their friend as well as their Savior.

Who are your friends? Follow Jesus in befriending the lost.

1. 1 Corinthians 1:27; James 2:5
2. Isaiah 40:55; Isaiah 7:12; Psalm 89:22-37; Psalm 45:3-5
3. Psalm 23
4. Richard L. Rohrbaugh, Bruce J. Malina, *Social Science Commentary on the Synoptic Gospels* (Fortress Press, 1993).
5. Mark 2:15
6. Luke 19:1-9
7. Proverbs 31:8-9
8. 1 John 4:4
9. Galatians 3:28

16

THE OPPOSITE SPIRIT

I was squirming. I was in a preparation seminar for people interested in ministering to men. "Racial prejudice is the issue," we were told. "If you are to make an impact on the nation, it's one of the seven key areas you'll need to address."

Finally, sitting there in a windswept cottage in the stark beauty of the Lake District, I interrupted. "The problem for English Christians is more likely to be class prejudice." I explained how the Evangelical church in the U.K. had been dominated for years by graduates of Oxford or Cambridge, and the English fee-paying elite schools. Their accents, their attitudes, and their wariness of all things American was an issue as far as I was concerned.

The grandson of a shipyard worker and acutely aware of the impact of the 1929 financial crash on my family circle and other working class people in Northern Ireland, I felt that over the years I had been marginalized by some because of my regional accent.

It was one of those moments where even as you are saying something you realize the prejudices of your own heart, and the mixture of hurt and prejudice that resides within you and masquerades as righteous indignation. I had to stop.

Moments later, another voice piped up across the room. He was the son of a military officer, educated in an elite school. He recounted his deep hurt at being mocked for his upper class accent and his feeling of alienation, even sometimes in church circles. The circle was closed. Two men, raised in different circumstances from different backgrounds, revealing the inner tensions they felt, but had often buried.

The prophets had spoken to themselves. In airing a problem, we had been convicted of our own anger. How much of my interactions with others were tainted by my slow burning anger?

But there is another question. How much of our contact as a Christian community with the wider culture is tainted by anger, not love, care, or compassion?

Not that we don't sometimes have reason to be mad. We may sometimes perceive ourselves as a minority, dismissed by the media as irrelevant, caricatured in popular entertainment and even in informal conversations as champions of positions we may not even hold.

Sometimes we're mad with everyone: ourselves, for not being good enough people, the Church, for not being hip enough, and the world, for despising us. It may well make us a little brittle and shrill.

It may even make us patronizing, dismissive, and deeply, profoundly suspicious of the motives, trustworthiness, and general attitude of anyone who is not a Christian. We speak our biblically sound words in our aggressive-defenders-of-the-truth voice, and people don't listen. But of course that isn't a problem, because it only confirms our view that we're living in a godless hard-hearted generation.

In the midst of it all, we may view life in tabloid headline terms.

Muslims are Muslims, Occultists are Occultists and Evangelicals
are Evangelicals. The reality is very different. Muslims have
two main branches: the Sunni and Shiites. The Sunni, like
Protestantism has many sub branches. The Wahhabi have an
austere, no frills view of life and are thought to have inspired
Bin Laden and many of the Al Qaeda terrorists. The Deobandi
school of religion underpinned the Taliban and, like the ancient
Pharisees, added multiple rules to their faith to help preserve
purity.

In the U.K., the Evangelical Alliance undertook a survey of
its membership and people from similar backgrounds. They
identified seventeen distinct sub groups. It's hard, therefore to
generalize about Evangelicals. Whatever they have in common
with respect to Jesus' life, death, and resurrection, they have vastly
different perspectives on the end-times, women in ministry, the
gifts of the Spirit, the nature of free will, and many other details.

In our town are many New Age followers, pagans, and satanists.
On the face of it, they are all occultists, but what would be true
of one group, would be totally untrue of another. A local pagan
leader, fond of his spell-casting ceremonies in high places and
general white-robe-wearing mystical behavior, is the most vocal
local critic of satanism. The Reiki healers who live in the streets
near us would likewise probably laugh at the idea of gathering
on a local hill near an ancient fertility symbol and dancing and
chanting.

The possibility of dialogue with any of them will evaporate if we
generalize about what they believe or dismiss their beliefs in a
sentence. They will soon remind us of the murderous behavior of
Christians in the Crusades or the bitter sectarian conflict on the
streets of Belfast. Suggesting that the Crusades was as much about
personal power as religion, that those who fight in Northern
Ireland are often godless gangsters who never darken the doors of
a church, and that Communism and Nazism has killed more than
114 million people in the last century, a much greater number
than those killed in religious conflict, will have little impact on

their minds if we've already generalized about their beliefs.

How can we retain a principled perspective but not act like bigots? How can we irritate people with truth, not a mean attitude? Jesus offers us several insights, which, if understood singly or together, will start to make a difference and help us "minister in the opposite spirit."

THROUGH JESUS' EYES

Sometimes the way we view people is a reflection of what we think the Bible says about them. We know from Scripture and experience that humankind can be fickle, hard-hearted, devious, and at times utterly selfish. It's not a big jump for us to then assume everyone who has not discovered Jesus is:

- Basically unhappy and messed up.
- Hostile to faith.
- Given to evil in every action.
- Incapable of goodness or unselfish behavior.

This breeds a superior attitude within us and perhaps even a messianic complex. "I will help these poor people discover the error of their spiritual ways."

The reality of life is actually a little different. People may be at any point on a spectrum of spiritual interest, from utter indifference and deliberate evil to active interest in Jesus.

Additionally, they may well be capable of good. Jesus certainly thought so, warning His listeners not to become proud, because even pagans love their friends and greet each other warmly.[1] Even evil fathers know how to give good gifts to their children.[2]

The Bible tells us we have been made in the image of God.[3] Sin has marred, muddied, distorted, and poisoned that within us, but it hasn't totally destroyed it. The ability to be good is a creational gift to us from God.

Christians have taken this possibility of goodness a step further by intentionally renouncing evil, saying sorry to God for past rebellion and orientating their lives toward the example of Jesus.

Street corner preachers who warn their listeners that they are sinners bound for hell will always be able to hold up a trophy conversion, usually of a previously churched person called back to the straight and narrow through guilt or fear. But for the large section of the population for whom life is a spiritual muddle, rather than a conscious minute-by-minute rebellion against God, it sounds like the posturing of the self-righteous.

The good works of the spiritual wanderer or the happy pagan do not earn them merit with God.[4] The fact that they recognize fragments of the truth and practice sporadic goodness merely reflects shards of the image of God, breaking through the shattered snapshot we see of their lives.

If we recognize that people will have grasped fragments of truth and invite them to discover more of it, we may find that people listen. They will still find it offensive, as they did when Paul talked to them of their gods and the Jesus who had risen from the dead, but many wanted to talk more. A simple dismissal of the local religious practices would have merely united the crowd against Paul.[5]

HUMILITY AND EMPATHY

Some of us struggle to approach people with humility because to admit that we have frailties to ourselves would throw us into paroxysms of guilt because we are not perfect. We may also project our anger with our imperfection onto others, denouncing that which troubles us.

Imperfection is a reality while we remain in this our earthly state, but a preacher I heard in Atlanta one time captured it well when he said: "I'm sure not the man I need to be, but I'm sure not the man I used to be."

Recognizing that we are a work in progress, moving intentionally toward a holy life will help us approach other "works in progress" with the right mixture of "I've been where you are" and "I can show you a better place to go." This may be reflected in something as simple as your language. Imagine you're talking to someone about sexual temptation. Using the word "you" throughout the conversation will position you as a spiritually superior person. Talking about we, us, and suggesting that some of the strategies you mention have helped you suggests that you're a fellow pilgrim offering help to someone who has stumbled.

You may also want to elicit the support of the Holy Spirit. It's as simple as asking for an understanding of the suffering people sometimes experience. I've asked for it. Get ready though. God often sneaks up on you unbidden and at times when you're not in a meeting or any religious gathering.

I look out over a meeting and feel the emotional anguish of a person in the crowd. I stand in church and find myself lost in the potential emotions of a girl from the home of a messy divorce. Sometimes I can walk past people in the street and feel stricken with emotion as the Spirit gives me insight into their life. Today I watched a women at a road junction, outwardly well dressed, but in reality slumped inside, sadness etched on her face.

Jesus felt these emotions as He wept over Jerusalem and is noted to have been moved with compassion as He comprehended the spiritual confusion in people's lives.[6]

Viewing people as sheep without a shepherd, rather than enemies of God will subtly affect your tone, body language, and patterns of speech. You'll not view them as enemies, but rather as people waiting to discover that they too can be a friend of God.

Jesus has more radical advice for us.

LIVING BY WISDOM

"Bless those who despitefully use you."[7] How irritating is that?

People talk about the hard sayings of Jesus. Well, wrestle with that one.

I once irritated an already irate friend by suggesting they simply give something to someone who had changed their mind about buying it as part of a house purchase. "Don't you quote Scripture at me," I was warned, before they dissolved into laughter, remembering that they had been among those who had taught me to honor the wisdom of the Bible.

Jesus doesn't hold back. "Love your enemies, bless them that curse you, do good to them that hate you, and pray for them which despitefully use you and persecute you."[8]

It seems counter intuitive to us. Forgive them perhaps—if they ask for forgiveness. Refrain from revenge or verbal attacks. We could handle that. But Jesus is looking for deliberate choices to be made: Bless them, do good, pray.

Our discipleship, our communication, our lives lived in the light of the example of the life of Christ is not a matter of behavior or sin management. It is rooted in our values. Our values shape our thinking, which in turn shapes our behavior.

Are we ready to make unrelenting grace a core value in our lives?

Jesus loved the enemy's servant who escorted Him to a false trial and a violent death. Attacked by an irate Peter with a sword, he was healed by a compassionate Jesus.[9]

Jesus is militant about peacemaking. He looks at hate from many angles.

Do good to them who hate you. Even as I write, it's hard to think how you would do this, and where you would find the emotional reserves. Jesus captures the possibility in His story of the merciful Samaritan who risks his own safety to preserve the life of a man from a race that hated his.

Following September 11, 2001, many churches approached their local mosques and made it clear that while they had no sympathy for the teaching of the Koran, they wanted no part in any violence, intolerance, or wild rhetoric about ordinary Muslim believers. In a San Diego church, people went shopping with their Arab neighbors, ready to stand alongside them should they receive any abuse. This simple act was a means of spiritual warfare against Satan. Any root of bitterness between the Christian and Muslim community produces distrust that will fester for generations. Letting another community know that although they are different and you have fundamental disagreements with them, you nevertheless bear them no animosity, is a powerful act of healing goodness.

In any community you might come into conflict with for whatever reason, there will be people with stories: stories of violence against them and stories of verbal abuse. Add to their personal hurt the folklore of conflict, season it with a fallen human nature, and you have a recipe for chronic unrest.

Simple acts of kindness can neutralize decades of bitterness by dismantling stereotypes and building a foundation for trust.

Jesus hasn't finished with us. He wants us to pray for our enemies.

As we come to pray for those who have wronged us or opposed us, a change is forced in our inner story about them. Think about this for a moment: God looks to His creation and offers the rebellious sinful people restoration. He establishes covenants with them through Noah, Abraham, Moses, and David. He spares cities because of the prayers of one man; He suggests time and again that He will hold back His judgment on an immoral or murderous generation, if they will turn their hearts toward Him. Finally, He sends His Son to teach of the kingdom and conquer sin and death on a hill outside Jerusalem.

In all of this, God believed in the possibility of change. Jesus gathered twelve men who needed change. Change in an impetuous fisherman named Peter, change in a doubting Thomas, change in a wary Nathaniel, change in an extremist Simon, and change in a compromised Matthew. As you come to pray for your enemies, you too will need that vision of hope, a belief that God can bring change to their lives.

It may help you to consider how you might pray. Often we ask God to thwart our enemies. We want him to destroy their plans, undermine their beliefs, and force them to admit the poverty of their ideas and lifestyle.

How about asking God to reveal His character to them? How could God resist the invitation to see His name honored because the beauty and goodness of the character is exhibited in a situation? I have prayed that God will reveal Himself as a loving Father and a gracious friend to a man in our circle of friends. He has had significant involvement in the occult at a fairly high level. It's tempting to simply pray that the powers of deception will no longer have a hold on his mind, and we do. But His occult dabbling was only a symptom of a deeper longing. He'll be really well when His heart understands the heart of God.

When you think about the apostles of anger or alienation in popular music in our culture, such as Marilyn Manson or Slipknot, Depeche Mode or the former Beatle, John Lennon, it's easy to know what you might pray against. But ask yourself this question. What is their anger a symptom of? What distorted view of God do they have?

Depeche Mode rose to a worldwide fame that lasted twenty years. Their roots were in a church youth group. In America particularly, they were regarded as a voice for an alienated generation. Others regarded them as a pernicious influence following the release of their "Blasphemous Rumours" and "Personal Jesus" singles.

So what happened to the innocent pop stars? They couldn't understand why their church urged people to pray for the sick and regularly announced their deaths. But what really sparked their spiritual diversion into darker paths was the death in a car accident of a friend who had committed her life to Christ only weeks before.

Their songs detonated a predictable barrage of criticism from rent-a-quote preachers rushing to the defense of the faith. Many would see the band's songs completely in isolation and perhaps reflect that once again "godless pop stars" were attacking "our faith." The reality was that their spiritual quest and personal idealism had run aground on the rocks of the problem of suffering and the nature of God's will. (To debate that here would take another book, but there are answers to these thorny problems— see *Is God to Blame* by Greg Boyd (IVP, 2003) for a provocative new look at this important subject.)

Praying for them and talking to them would have been much more productive than praying and campaigning against them.

This is reinforced elsewhere in Scripture. The writer of the Proverbs reminds us that a "gentle answer turns away wrath."[10] Paul, as he instructs Timothy, is quite emphatic about our demeanor.[11] We are not to quarrel or harbor resentment. Those who oppose us are to be gently instructed. Paul is not talking about accommodation or compromise, simply attitude and tone.

Jesus had also instructed His followers to practice a form of behavior that exhibited neither weakness nor antagonism, and left us with a memorable image of turning the other cheek, a line that surfaced in The Black Eyed Peas' chart-topping "Where is the Love," even as this chapter was being written.

Jesus tells His disciples to turn the other cheek, to carry loads for an extra mile, and to give those who demand your tunic your cloak as well.

Striking someone on the cheek with a slap was an insult. They would struggle to hit you again with the back of their hand if you turned the other cheek. They would be reluctant to use their traditionally "unclean" hand to hit you or to simply punch. To do so would be to admit to them that you were their social equal. It was also highly likely in the Mediterranean world of Jesus' time that this would all take place in public, and bystanders would immediately intervene.[12] Allowing others to defend you allows for future reconciliation and undermines the possible escalation of the dispute into a demand for satisfaction and violent feuding.

Being obliged to carry the load for another, often a Roman soldier, but offering to take it a second, places them in a difficult position. They too are bound by a code that suggests they can oblige people to help them, but they can't abuse that power.

Jesus calls His disciples to defuse situations of potential conflict by avoiding anger and remaining resolute, helpful, or generous. None of these are positions of weakness.

The wisdom we need will find expression in patterns of thinking. Jesus, through the aid of the Holy Spirit and the provocation of the Word of God, wants to change the pattern of our thinking.[13]

We often hear the words "love your enemy" and feel a pang of guilt. We quickly embark on some emotional management exercises. The Bible is often not very good at backing up this type of spiritual self-punishment. The Psalmists wails and rants about his need for deliverance, but affirms his trust in God.[14] There is, however, an emotional transparency about his song. The Apostle in his letter to the Ephesians reminds them to "be angry and sin not."[15]

Jesus and the other Bible writers want us to respond to our enemies in the light of our convictions, not our emotions. And they want our convictions to be rooted in the belief that the God who called the proud but murderous Paul to follow Him and help shape the Church can touch the lives of any we regard as our enemies.

Will you follow Jesus in being a peacemaker and reconciler?

1. Matthew 5:46-47
2. Luke 11:11.
3. Genesis 1:26
4. Ephesians 2:8-10
5. Acts 17:16-32
6. Luke 19:41, Mark 6:34
7. Matthew 5:44
8. Luke 6:27-28
9. Luke 22:49-51
10. Proverbs 15:1
11. 2 Timothy 2:24-26
12. Richard L. Rohrbaugh, Bruce J. Malina, *Social Science Commentary on the Synoptic Gospels* (Fortess Press, 1993).
13. Romans 12:2
14. Psalm 13
15. Ephesians 4:16

17

THE TRICKLE UP THEORY

You can't study world history for long without discovering the
role of religion in the affairs of humanity. Adherents.com lists the
key world religions as follows:

Christianity	2 billion
Islam	1.3 billion
Hinduism	900 million
Buddhism	360 million
Judaism	14 million

Only 850 million people in an estimated world population
of 6 billion have identified themselves as having no religion
whatsoever.

It's clear from the current affairs programs of our day that religion
plays a major role in the lives of our nations. The Saudi nobility
fund the spread of Islamic education. British Prime Minister Tony
Blair is quizzed as to whether he prays with George W. Bush at
political summits. The Christian Right are regarded as a force in
American politics, while various Christian Democrat parties are
influential in Europe.

Christians seek to influence the governments of our nations. Some seek a simple "voice at the table of public debate." Others seek legislative power, not merely to protect the faithful or restrain evil, but to promote a legislative agenda.

But many Christians feel some affinity for those who protest the arms trade with the phrase "not in my name." Is all that is done in the name of Christ or Christians in the political arena reflective of biblical truth or your own perspective on biblical principle? How important is it for us to have our hands on the levers of power?

Until the time of the Roman Emperor Constantine it wasn't really an issue. The Greco-Roman view of divinity reigned supreme and it was often the Emperor who was worshiped. Christianity was a persecuted religion, caught between the disapproval of Jewish religious leaders around the world and the followers of the local gods.

Constantine offered the Church the protection of the State. He helped convene early church councils, which were formed to establish the basic creeds of our faith, such as the Nicene creed. Church communities breathed a sigh of relief and emerged from their sometimes secretive world. It was not to be the fresh start many anticipated.

The Church had taken great pains to ascertain that the faith of the new convert was genuine and life-transforming. Now they faced a situation where the Christian religion was identified with national structures, and many considered themselves Christian, regardless of their relationship with God and the reality of a transformed life.

The temptation of power and control still influences the Church in all its complexity and diversity. Here's the scenario: Wouldn't it be good if prominent figures in society were Christians? Politicians, musicians, and sports figures. It gives the message of the Church credibility. We need to invest a great deal of energy into this; otherwise the Church will appear marginal and ineffective and people will not take our message seriously.

It's half-true, and all the more damaging as a result. There is absolutely no harm in people of faith being creative and passionate about how a nation is governed or committed to sporting excellence. The profile of such people can create a "trickle down" climate of influence and lend Christian faith plausibility.

But the Saudi Christian or the persecuted Christian believer in a Hindu community in India hasn't got the luxury of the social prestige derived from the influence of Christian figures in society.

The power of a passionate Christian community will always outweigh any "high profile believer" influence in the life of an individual. God's chosen instrument of change, the means by which His Holy Spirit can bring the message of Jesus, is us. God uses communities of believers to effect change. God has a trickle up theory. He can change a country from the bottom up, street by street, house by house, heart by heart.

When a heart is changed, a family changes. Changed families create changed communities. Changed communities create justice and harmony and influence the very atmosphere of a nation.

LET'S GET PROVOCATIVE NOW
If we were in power, would we be able to help a nation become fully devoted followers of Jesus? How would we do that? Do systems of control, except when used to restrain what is recognized as evil by a society, do anything more than spark resentment and rebellion?

Can we legislate morality if people are not passionately committed to the value system we hold?

Tough questions. What is to be our response? Should we retreat into our Christian groups and have nothing to say about the life of our society? How are we to relate to those in power? How does a Christian community make a different within the wider communities in which it finds itself?

We can discover the answers by exploring the following:

- What can Jesus teach us about relating to those in power?
- What is the importance of family structures for societal transformation?
- How does the Church influence the rest of society?
- What is the proper role of tolerance in our lives, in our churches and, and within society?

JESUS AND POWER

Jesus wasn't intimidated by power. Jesus valued people more than rules and both in words and deeds showed Himself willing to "speak the truth to power."

Four examples will suffice, but His life is littered with examples.

One of His earliest healings was of a leper. He touched him in direct contradiction of the religious conventions of the day. It was an act of compassion, but also of defiance.[1]

Jesus did not tailor His message or His actions to win the approval of the crowd. As He entered Jericho, He singled out Zacchaeus and invited Himself to his home. This would have outraged the political zealots because of the tax collector's links with the Romans. The priests would have been offended because Zacchaeus was from an unclean profession. The ordinary man would have been shocked that Jesus would extend friendship to a man who was exploiting them.[2]

A willingness to proclaim the truth, whatever the power brokers thought, was evidenced when Jesus made His first major contribution to synagogue life in Nazareth. He stood and read the words of Isaiah 61 and reminded His listeners that He had come to release the oppressed. The people began to flatter Him with their praise, but He steeled Himself and told them that they were hard hearted. The crowd was angry enough to contemplate killing Him.[3]

As Jesus entered Jerusalem prior to the events that would lead to His death, He engaged in a relentless confrontation of the powers that governed religious life. He entered the temple courts and sought to drive out those who were making it expensive for the ordinary people to worship and make their sacrifices. The next day, He was challenged as to the source of His authority. He asked a question about the authority of John the Baptist, which stumped His accusers and then drove the point home by telling the story of the two sons. One promises to serve but doesn't; the other declines to serve but does. Jesus made it clear that the despised tax collectors and prostitutes werre proving to be the ones who decide to serve. Jesus may not have used inflammatory language, but He seemed content to use incendiary metaphors when challenging the power structures of His day.[4]

If we are to follow Jesus, we will have to be ready to speak the truth to power.

JESUS RESISTED THE OFFER OF STRUCTURAL POWER

Part of the disappointment some felt about Jesus related to their expectation of a Messiah who would bring political freedom and deliver them from the Romans. When He reflected more of the values of the suffering servant of Isaiah 53, their disappointment was marked.

Jesus made a point of rejecting conventional power throughout His time on earth. He was looking for personal revolutions, not changes of government. His first refusal of power is noted during the time of temptation in the wilderness. The second temptation was a specific invitation to worship the devil and receive the kingdoms of the world. Jesus rejected the offer, reminding the tempter that worship is only to be given to the Lord God.[5]

Having been tempted by the devil, Jesus became the subject of popular acclaim by the crowd following the feeding of the five thousand. Believing Him to be the "prophet long awaited," they were likely to make Him king by force. This was not the path He had chosen, and He withdrew into the mountains by Himself.[6]

At the time of His greatest need, or when facing the greatest rejections, Jesus could have called on the creative power that put the universe in place. He refused to use power in this way. He rejected the idea of sending fire raining down onto a Samaritan village in John.[7] But most telling is Jesus' rejection of the violence of His disciples. He rebuked Peter for attacking the High Priest's servant with a sword. He reminded those who had come to arrest Him that He was not leading an armed rebellion, that His death would have a purpose, and that if He wished to escape it, He could have asked the Father for twelve thousand angels.[8]

Jesus rejected the idea of power as a means of societal change. He was plotting a revolution of the heart, not of the sword.

JESUS DIDN'T DESPISE POWER

Those who are suspicious of power and the interests that seek to use it for their own purposes might regard Jesus as an ally, given His fearless prophetic stance and studied disregard for conventional power structures.

But a holy paradox emerges again as we study His life. Jesus would not embrace conventional power, but He did not despise or reject those who held some form of power. The Scriptures record Him in dialogue with Nicodemus and mention His friendship with Joseph of Arimathea. Both were members of the Council of the Jews, a key body in the uneasy relationship with the Romans.[9]

Later Scriptures call for prayer for those in authority and encourage people to endure hardship with patience, rather than resorting to disobedience or anarchy. Christians are given an example of a prophetic man, Jesus, leading a prophetic community that will do good regardless of a person's position in society and against the flow of conventional tradition. But Jesus will not pursue "the power of the sword" as a means to help bring spiritual compliance in society.

So how can followers of Jesus influence their society and speak of Jesus' values to the wider culture?

BECOMING THE VOICE OF A COMMUNITY

Following Jesus is rarely a single act. It's many small acts that combine to make a large difference. If we are to be voices for and within our communities, we will need to embrace several principles that will together help make those who call themselves Christians be a redemptive community.

THE FAMILY, CLAN, AND TRIBE

The Bible is orientated toward preserving the bonds of family, clan, and tribe. The Jubilee regulations which provided for land to be returned after fifty years were meant to ensure that successive generations were not condemned to servitude and poverty because of the mistakes of one man. The Ten Commandments call on us to honor our fathers and mothers, an invitation to not merely thank them for their early nurture of us, but to ensure their needs are met in later life. Biblical injunctions about sex outside of marriage, adultery, and the obligation of men to marry the widows of their brothers, all relate to the underlying wisdom of God's creational intent and His desire to preserve family, kinship, and personal land and property, as a means whereby people can find stability, support, and sustenance.

If you want to follow Jesus, you will want to consider how the government of your nation regards the family and personal property. You will also want to embody or bring your values to life within your church community.

OUR STEWARDSHIP OF CREATION

The activity of humankind has a major impact on the land. This term, which often means the literal soil but can be used to speak of geographical regions is very common in Scripture, which refers to it more than 1,700 times.

The spiritual logic is this: When people live according to God's wisdom, the land flourishes. The simplistic interpretation of this would suggest that God blesses people as a deliberate act on His part. While God can clearly do this it's also worth noting that the blessing sometimes occurs because people are working in harmony with God's created purpose. How does this work?

It can work in multiple ways. A man or woman who works hard and diligently will become a figure of trust and be given extra responsibility or business as a result. Someone who becomes a Christian and gives up an alcohol dependence or drug habit will discover they have more money and a renewal of hope and purpose in their life.

In a direct and literal way, Christians who regard the earth as the Lord's and believe God rejoiced over the goodness of it when He made it will take seriously the Genesis 2:15 injunction to take care of it. They'll view with concern any activity that pollutes it or, because of chemical or biological manipulation, causes it to become toxic. This is not the place to reflect at any length on a Christian perspective on environmental issues, but suffice it to say that our silence allows those who worship the earth rather than its Maker to steal our prophetic thunder.

Scripture invites us to care for the earth and also reminds us we will be the "repairer of broken walls, and restorers of streets." Scripture often locates people in terms of their town or city. Jesus of Nazareth, Simon of Cyrene, Saul of Tarsus.

Our ability to bring transformation in a local society will directly relate to how much we actually care for that place. We are God's agents of influence there. But if we only "sleep" there rather than "live" there, we won't be those who become trusted within that community.

TRUST AND INFLUENCE

Our ability to influence will be directly related to our willingness to let our lives be Christ-like in four different contexts.

THE FAMILY OR KINSHIP GROUP
This is the place where we are known best. Christians have traditionally valued family and kin.

THE WORKPLACE
Some Christians regard work as a necessary evil, a means to earn money to give to the Church and feed the family. Work in the Church is regarded as a higher calling.

The priesthood of all believers is an idea found throughout the New Testament which will help us to respond to this distorted view.[10] This concept, allied with the idea that we are stewards of creation, gives us a new perspective on work. Our work is part of our sacrifice to God; it's an act of worship, whereby we express our faith by serving others, seeking to be excellent and creating products and services that enable society to continue and flourish.

The workplace is not simply a place to "evangelize," but an arena where we can simply be Christ-like. The ministry gifts of Ephesians 4:11 will come into play in the workplace, just as they do within the gathered congregation. A person with a pastor's heart will become trusted as a confidant and comfort. A teacher will show gifts of communication. A person with apostolic character will show leadership abilities.

OUR FRIENDSHIP CIRCLE
In all of our lives, there may be people with whom we associate in clubs or projects, hobbies or common interests. They may be people whom we have known since childhood or met as students. For some Christians, this group is made up entirely of other Christians. When this happens, our light is being hidden under a bushel. The influence of our character is not being felt in the wider social networks of our town or neighborhood. It is here that the biblical metaphor of "salt and light" comes to its fullest expression.[11]

There has to be a willingness on our part to invest time in the lives of others. We need to expect to continue to love and respect them whether they respond to our message or not. We will also need to get over any residual guilt about the idea of enjoying ourselves in activities that do not have overt spiritual overtones.

OUR NEIGHBORHOOD
We can't be best friends with everyone. Jesus had one close friend, two others in His inner circle, and twelve in His overall team. He had at least seventy-two other followers, and as many as 500 counted themselves as among His adherents. There will be many people in your town among your 500. You may not know them well, but they will be aware of you and perhaps even admire you. Your stance and character will act as a spiritual weathervane to them, pointing them in the direction the wind of the Holy Spirit blows. Simple greetings and small kindnesses will speak volumes.

THE CHURCH AS MEDIATOR
The vast majority of people in our societies often feel powerless. They don't believe they can challenge the powerful, seek justice, or stop injustice. They feel insignificant. The church community in this context can help them feel empowered by acting as a place of hope and a mediating structure between the small family and the monolithic state.

So how can the Christian co-exist within that state alongside a variety other belief systems?

Here are three principles that may help us:

THE PRINCIPLE OF TOLERANCE
This reflects a belief that people should be free to pursue any religious practice that is not against the law of the land and the common sense ethical base upon which that law often rests. Christians will not seek to legislate against the everyday practices of others or use the power of the state to enforce a specific religion as the national state religion.

THE PRINCIPLE OF SOCIAL TOLERANCE
This means we will not shun people who don't share our

perspective. In fact, we will make a special effort to get to know them. This strikes at the root of racism and other forms of social hostility and reflects the belief that those made in the image of God deserve to be treated with dignity whatever their belief system.

THE PRINCIPLE OF INTELLECTUAL VITALITY

Defending the right of others to believe what they believe and treating them with dignity does not mean we have to make an accommodation with their ideas or forgo expressing ours lest they be offended. We're not looking for the common ground. We're simply seeking to express our views with a degree of grace and preserve the right to debate that will allow us to participate in the spiritual dialogues of our towns and cities.

Following Jesus will require us to examine our attitudes toward power and influence and to embrace the way of the humble, the way of the powerless, and the way of The Servant King. The hands that flung stars into space washed the disciples' feet. The hands that could hold the dust of the earth as if it were a mere speck were nailed to a tree. The commander of legions of angels chooses to die that we might live. He defied convention to win the hearts of multitudes.

It's time to follow Jesus.

1. Matthew 8:3
2. Luke 19:1-10
3. Luke 4:14-30
4. Matthew 21:12-32
5. Luke 4:5-8
6. John 6:14-15
7. Luke 9:51-56
8. Matthew 26:50-56
9. John 3
10. 1 Peter 2:9
11. Matthew 5:13-14

FOLLOWING
JESUS

Following Jesus will mean that you can:

Seek a holiness that is expressed in goodness to others, joy in God's creation, and a belief that He wants you to be fully human.

Question belief systems that use Jesus to advance the social conventions of the day—they may be true, but then again, maybe not.

Embrace the possibility that Jesus could be both compassionate and wild and that the Bible shows us many both/and paradoxes that may challenge our neat either/or categories.

Become aware that your whole life is a learning experience and that you discover Jesus everywhere, not just in church.

Discover that the Bible is a rich book, full of wisdom, history, poetry, and story.

Find that a story speaks to the emotions in a way that a one-line statement of truth may never do.

Take risks and learn from your failure rather than trying to engineer a perfect unspoiled life.

Discover solutions for today in the wisdom and practice of the Church fathers of the last two millennia.

Find your spiritual rhythm from the small and large traditions that mean God is onstage in your theater of waking dreams.

Find a life that models Christ-likeness to you for the here and now.

Seek out the everyday spiritual disciplines that will comfort your heart and feed your mind.

Enjoy the five senses God gave you and revel in them even as you worship Him.

Follow Him with thankfulness, laying aside the dead weight of obligation and disinterested duty.

Try to make sense of the world, using the mind He gave you and the wisdom revealed to the patriarchs, to the prophets, and through Jesus.

Embrace the broken and the lost, the losers and the freaks, the marginalized and the insignificant as an act of worship and a refection of the Father's heart.

Find a new way of relating to your enemies.

Permeate creation with the goodness of God as you and your friends become a redemptive community.

Let the learning begin …

Get a FREE ISSUE of
RELEVANT magazine!
God. life. progressive culture.